ESSENTIAL CONCEPTS

Music Reading for Keyboard

THE COMPLETE METHOD

by Larry Steelman

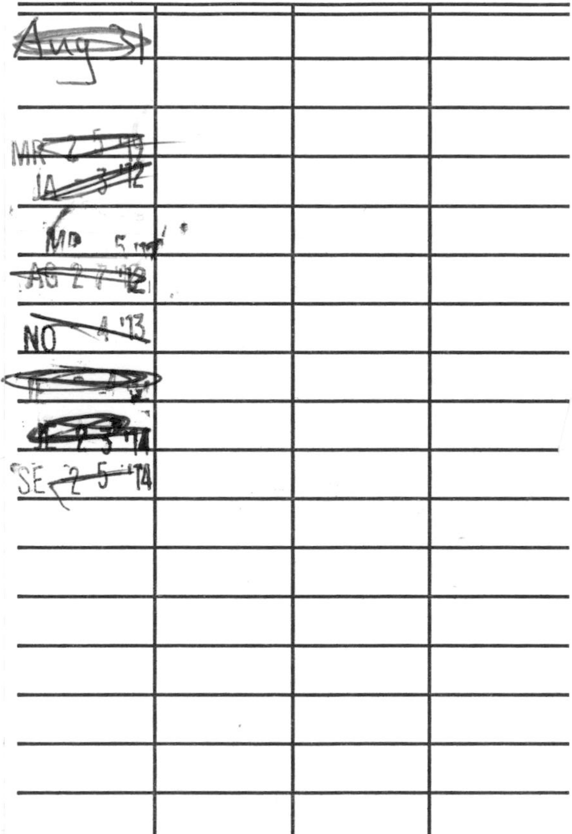

ISBN 0-7935-8200-8

HAL•LEONARD®
CORPORATION
7777 W. BLUEMOUND RD. P.O. BOX 13819 MILWAUKEE, WI 53213

Visit Hal Leonard Online at
www.halleonard.com

Table of Contents

Introduction

People enter the world of music through listening; it's pure enjoyment and need not involve much knowledge about how things work. When one wants to learn more about how music works, however, one must learn the language. The study of music reading allows a student to try out music quickly and absorb it faster. It also allows a musician to translate his or her own ideas so that other people can play and enjoy them.

In this book, we will learn a step-by-step method of reading music that breaks down the process into manageable chunks. We'll start by learning the basic concepts of music reading—pitch, rhythm, meter, clefs, key signatures, repeat signs, etc.—and drilling those concepts with exercises in rhythm and pitch. Very quickly, we'll begin learning actual tunes and making those the focus of our study. The general idea will be to isolate each individual component of a piece of music so that we can perfect it before we have to combine that component with others. Specifically, we'll adopt a five-step approach to reading music:

- Examine the musical road map (repeat signs, multiple endings, D.C.s, D.S.s, codas, etc.).
- Find complicated rhythmic passages, and work them out.
- Read each note without the rhythm, in steady quarter notes.
- Play the notes and rhythms together, one hand at a time.
- Play the piece in its entirety with both hands together, at a comfortable tempo.

Of course, we'll explore these steps much further in the chapters to follow, and we'll apply them to tunes in a variety of popular styles—from rock and R&B to jazz and Latin.

As you work through the tunes and exercises in each chapter, be aware of the tempos you set; they should be just fast enough to challenge you, but not so fast that they frustrate you or cause excessive mistakes. This book is based on an MI class in which each chapter corresponds to a week's lesson. You should find that each chapter can be easily mastered in one week's time, particularly if you make it part of a regular practice routine. With regular practice, you can work on gradually increasing your tempos throughout each week. Always use a metronome so that you can measure your progress as you read a piece of music.

Above all, as you make your way through these lessons, I encourage you to think of sightreading as a way to free yourself rather than as work or drudgery. It does take practice and patience, but you can open up so many new experiences if you learn to read well.

Enough with the theoretical explanations, let's get started...

Larry Steelman

Chapter One

1

The Staff

First let's look at the musical *staff.* It is made up of five horizontal lines and four spaces. The first symbol at the left of a staff is called the *clef sign.* We will begin our reading studies in the *treble clef,* or *G clef.* It is called "the G clef" because the lower part of the symbol surrounds the second line of the staff, which represents the note G. Notice also the two numbers to the right of the treble clef—this is the *time signature.* The top number lets us know how many beats there are in each measure, and the second number, the one on the bottom, tells us the basic rhythmic unit. In this case, the time signature is 4/4 (four beats to the measure, with the quarter note representing one beat).

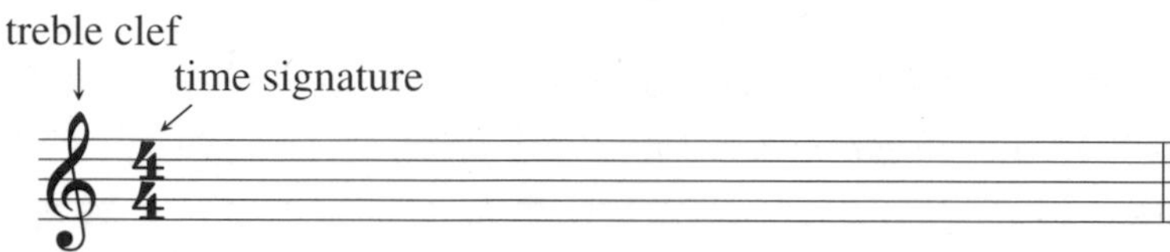

Notes

The note located on the bottom line of the treble clef is the E above middle C on the keyboard. From the bottom to the top, the notes on the lines are E, G, B, D, and F. The notes in the spaces are F, A, C, and E.

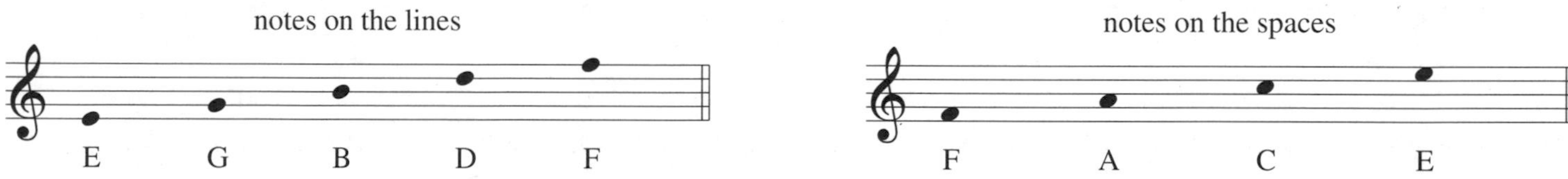

There are many cute ways of remembering these note names (Every Good Boy Does Fine, FACE, etc.). You may also count up from the bottom note E. It's OK if you have to use one of these methods at first, but try to discard such a crutch as soon as you can. It will just slow you down.

Rhythms

The next area to consider is the timing of the notes. In a time signature of 4/4, a note that lasts the whole measure is called a *whole note,* one that lasts half the measure is a *half note,* one that lasts a quarter of the measure is a *quarter note,* and one that lasts an eighth of the measure is called an *eighth note.* You get the idea.

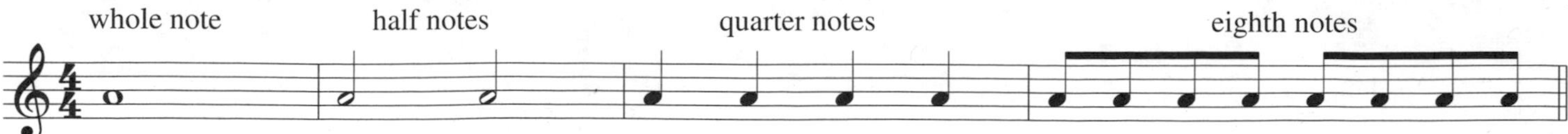

Rhythm Study

Now that we have some new knowledge, let's put it into practice. First, we will try some rhythm examples. Along with playing or clapping rhythms, we will learn to say syllables that correspond to the note values:

- For a whole note, say "1." You may tap your foot for the remaining beats, but you don't need to say anything for any rhythm that doesn't have a note attached.
- For two half notes, say "1" and "3." You may also whisper the missing beats if you wish (e.g. say "1," whisper "2," say "3," whisper "4").
- For four quarter notes, say "1, 2, 3, 4." If there were quarters on beats 1, 3, and 4, you could either whisper "2" or not do anything but tap your foot for that beat.
- For eighth notes, say the number of the beat or "and." Eight eighth notes, for instance, would sound like this: "1-and, 2-and, 3-and, 4-and."

Give a four-beat count-off, then play or clap the following rhythm exercise, vocalizing the note values. Try to keep a steady tempo. If you find that you have to slow down, your count-off was probably too fast.

Note Study

Exercises that work on note recognition skills will not involve rhythm. You should, however, give yourself a four-beat count-off and keep a steady tempo.

Chapter Two

2

2/4 Meter

We've already looked at 4/4 time, now let's look at another very common time signature: 2/4. We know from the previous chapter that the top number of a time signature represents the number of beats in each measure—in this case, two—while the bottom number represents the type of note that receives a beat—namely, the quarter note. We would therefore expect to see two quarter notes, or their equivalent, in each measure of 2/4.

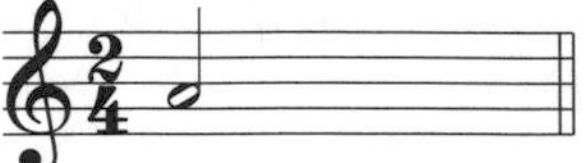

In the last chapter, we worked with exercises that placed notes *on* the beat; there were no syncopations or other complicated rhythms. In this chapter, we will use *ties* to make the examples a bit more rhythmically difficult. Ties simply extend a note by the value of the notes that follow it. Keep in mind that a tied note is always connected to another note *of the same pitch.* Notes of differing pitches are connected by *slurs.*

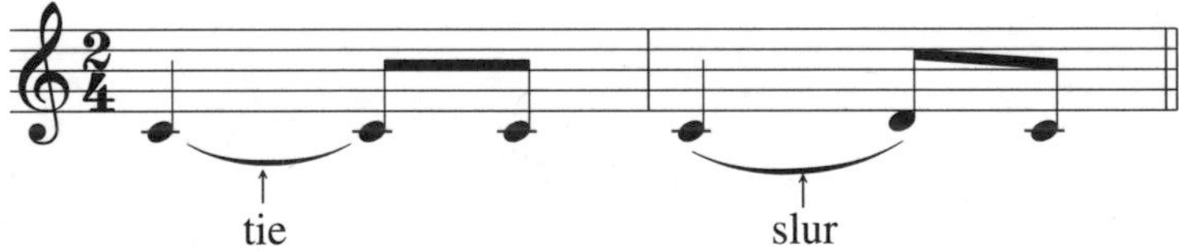

Rhythm Study

When vocalizing rhythms involving a tied note, do not say a syllable for the second note of the pair—only the note that is struck should receive a syllable.

Note Study

We won't examine any new information in this area, but we will extend our reading range to G above the treble staff.

For Further Practice

Create your own rhythm and note studies here.

Rhythm Study

Note Study

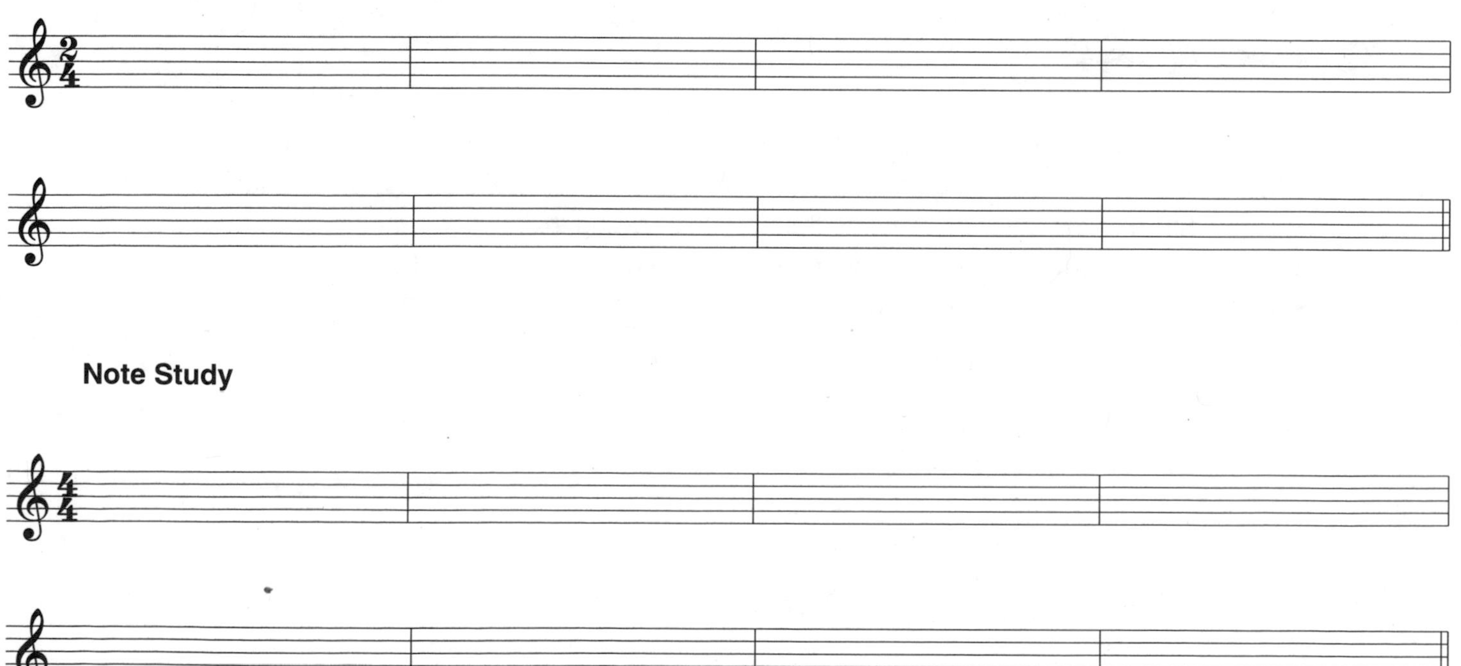

Chapter Three

3

3/4 Meter and Dotted Note Values

We've looked at 4/4 and 2/4 time signatures; now let's look at a time signature that cannot be divided by two: 3/4. In 3/4 time, there are three beats per measure, and the quarter note receives one beat. This means that, instead of a whole note or half note filling up a measure, a half note plus a quarter note is required. To write this value without using a tie, we need to use a *dotted note value.* A *dot* adds half the value of a note to any note that it follows. For instance, a dot following a half note adds a quarter note's value to the half, a dot following a quarter note adds an eight note's value to the quarter, and a dot following an eight note adds the value of a sixteenth to the eighth.

Bass Clef

So far, we have been working exclusively in the treble, or G, clef, but there are several other clefs commonly used in music. One is the *bass clef* (or *F clef*). The two dots of the bass clef enclose the fourth line from the bottom of the staff, designating the note F. Knowing this, we can deduce the other pitches. The top line is A, the third line is D, the second line from the bottom is B, and the bottom line is G. The spaces from the bottom up are A, C, E, and G.

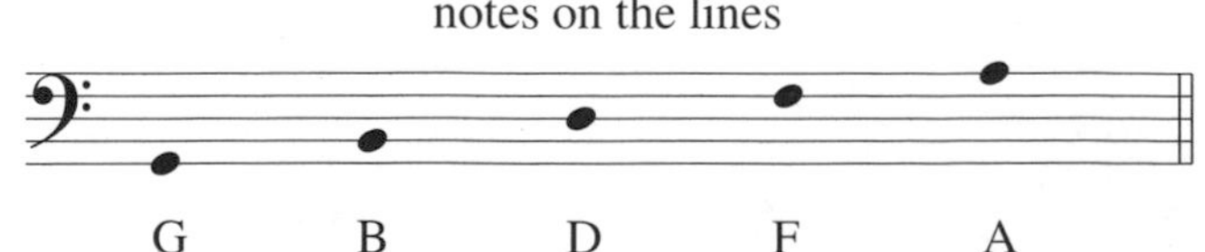

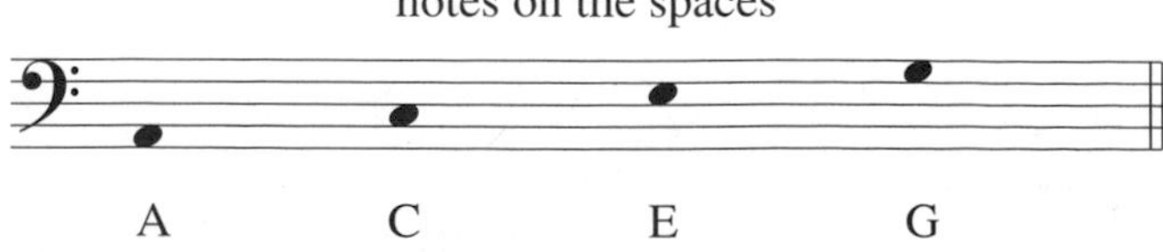

Rhythm Study

Note Study

Pentatonic Tune in C

Now let's apply our reading skills to a tune. This one is simple and repetitive enough that it should not require extensive preparation. Just take it at a slow tempo. (The tempo indication, ♩=112, is actually a performance tempo, not a sightreading tempo.) Notice that melody is stated first in the treble clef and then restated, almost verbatim, in the bass clef.

Chapter Four

4

Repeat Signs

We use *repeat signs* when we want to indicate that a certain section of music should be played twice before going on to the next section. Generally, repeats signs occur in pairs, at the beginning and end of the affected section; sometimes, however, when the first section of a song is to be repeated, the repeat signs at the beginning are omitted. The meaning is the same. Never use repeat signs inside other repeat signs—this is too confusing. Repeat signs can, however, be used in two sections next to each other.

Here are some acceptable and unacceptable examples of repeat signs.

Rhythm Study

Watch for the time changes in this exercise.

Note Study

Simple 3/4 Tune

Here's a simple melody in 3/4 time. Watch for the change from treble to bass clefs, and back again. Observe the repeat indications, and keep your tempo steady throughout.

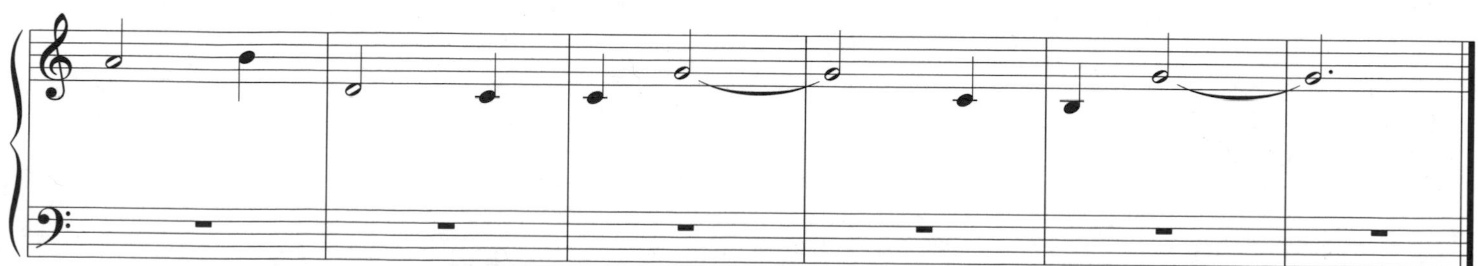

Chapter Five

5

Key Signatures and Accidentals

Until now, we have been avoiding anything but the "white" notes of the keyboard. Let's branch out a bit and expand our repertoire of pitches.

A *key signature,* found just to the right of the clef sign in a piece of music, tells us to play certain notes either *sharp* (one half step higher) or *flat* (one half step lower), compared to their pitch in a natural state. These sharps or flats apply throughout an entire piece—unless an accidental is used to temporarily cancel their effect. *Accidentals* are sharps, flats, or naturals that occur *within a specific measure.* They apply only to the measure in which they appear, with the affected notes reverting to their previous state when the next measure begins. (Notes in other octaves are not affected.) If a note with an accidental is tied to an adjoining measure, the accidental stays in effect only until the tied value runs out; the very next note is not affected by the former accidental.

Let's try some examples.

Note Study

Watch for the key signature changes, and observe the accidentals in this exercise.

Rhythm Study

Let's try working both hands simultaneously. First, go through this rhythm study with the right hand, then with the left. Finally, put both hands together. Keep the tempo comfortable and steady.

Swing Tune in C

This chapter, we have our first two-handed tune. Don't try to do everything at once; you'll want to prepare yourself for this piece.

- First, look at the rhythms. This tune has a boogie-woogie-type left-hand pattern with a less active right hand. Treat this like a rhythm study: practice the rhythm of the right hand alone first, then the left hand, then put the two together (all without the pitches).
- Second, look at the pitches. Take the right hand alone first. Treat this like a note study: play even quarter notes at a steady tempo. Don't slow down or speed up. Then take the left hand alone, once again keeping a steady tempo. It doesn't matter if it is slow as long as you keep it steady.
- Third, put the pitches and rhythms together, one hand at a time. First play the right hand, then the left.
- Finally, play both hands together. If you make mistakes, keep plugging along. You can try again after your first time and fix things then, but if you stop to repair things, and you are playing in an ensemble, the rest of the players will leave you in the dust.

Notice the tempo marking, in particular the *swing* (♫ = ♩♪ with triplet 3) indication. We'll explore the meaning of this notation later. For now, just play the tune as you see fit. Have fun with it!

Chapter Six

6

Endings

In Chapter 4, we introduced repeat signs. Often when we use repeat signs, we also make use of *multiple endings*. With multiple endings, the first repeat sign has one or several measures before it that have a bracket above them with a number, and additional measures after it that are also bracketed and numbered. The numbers tell us when to use specific endings. For instance, the most common use would be a first ending above the first repeat, then a second ending above the next measure. This would tell us to play to the first repeat, go back to the beginning, then play until the first ending, skipping over that ending to play through the second ending before continuing.

Most of the time, first and second endings are enough to organize a chart, but sometimes third, fourth, or even more endings are needed.

Rhythm Study

We have some challenging two-handed rhythms in our tune this chapter. Here is an exercise to help get you ready. Watch for the meter changes.

Note Study

These notes are drawn from the tune at the end of this chapter—first the notes of the right hand, then the notes of the left.

Waltz in F Minor

The previous rhythm and note studies should ensure that you are well-prepared to take on this tune. Once again, try playing each hand separately before you put both hands together.

Chapter Seven

7

Signs (𝄋) and Capos

We have looked at repeat signs and first and second endings as a way to organize a piece of music. Now let's look at few more organizing instructions. The *Sign* (𝄋) and its complement, *Dal Segno* (often abbreviated *D.S.*), tell us to return to the (𝄋) from wherever the Dal Segno instruction is given. If no other instructions are indicated, we would assume that all repeats and any first and second endings would be taken. A common variation on this instruction is *Dal Segno al Fine.* This tells us that after we take the "Dal Segno," we should play until we see the word "Fine," which indicates the end of the piece.

Still another instruction is *Da Capo*, or *D.C.* This literally means "from the head," referring to the beginning of the piece. When we see this instruction, we go back to the first measure and play until the Fine sign or the end of the piece.

In this first example, you would play to the last measure, where you would see the instruction D.S. al Fine, then return to measure 3 (𝄋) and play to the Fine sign in measure 5.

In this second example, you would play to the last measure, where you would see the instruction D.C. al Fine, then return to the beginning and play to the Fine sign.

Rhythm Study

The rhythms here will touch on many of the same rhythms contained in this chapter's tune. Watch out for those time signature changes.

Note Study

These pitches will also help prepare you for the tune to follow—first the right hand, then the left.

Rock Tune in B♭

This is actually more of a folk polka than a rock tune... In any case, read through the right hand first, then the left, then put both hands together, and take it at a moderate tempo. Observe the D.S. al Fine indication.

Chapter Eight

Codas

Last chapter, we looked at how to use signs (𝄋) and the instructions D.S. (Dal Segno) and D.C. (Da Capo). We also looked at the term Fine. In this chapter, we are going to add one more organizational tool: the instruction *To Coda* and its accompanying coda sign (𝄌).

When we reach a D.S. or D.C., we may also see the instruction D.S. al Coda, or D.C. al Coda. These instructions mean that when we return to the sign or to the beginning of the piece, we will play until we see a measure with the phrase "To Coda 𝄌" above it. We will then proceed to the section that has a coda sign (𝄌) above the first measure. This way, the coda signs in the repeated section and the new section link the two sections together. Here's a short example:

Rock Tune in B♭—Extended

This chapter, we'll forego rhythm and note studies in favor of returning to last chapter's tune—in an expanded form. Observe the Coda indication in this version.

To Coda
D.C. al Coda
Coda

Chapter Nine

9

Sixteenth-Note Rhythms

In the last eight chapters, we worked primarily with whole notes, half notes, quarter notes, and eighth notes. We'll now take a look at the next smallest rhythmic value: the *sixteenth note.* Its value is half that of the eighth; in other words, you will find four sixteenth notes in the space of two eighth notes.

We have seen that the syllables for eighth notes are the number of the beat plus an "and." For sixteenth notes, we will have to insert two more syllables: the syllable "e" (pronounced "ee") and the syllable "a" (pronounced "uh").

There is a technique for figuring out how to perform sixteenth-note rhythms that I like to call the *"shrink to fit" principle.* We have worked on all the combinations possible using eighth notes in a two-beat chunk. These include the following:

The same rhythmic units can be performed with sixteenth notes. All you have to do is "shrink" each two-beat group to one beat and use the new syllables. It's really the same rhythm played in half time. (In other words, if you cut the tempo in half, a one-beat pattern sounds the same as a two-beat pattern at the original tempo.) Compare this to the previous example:

Rhythm Study

This exercise should give you plenty of practice in playing sixteenths. Take it at a slow, steady tempo, and don't forget to articulate the rhythms with syllables.

Note Study

Watch the key signatures (and the accidentals) in this exercise.

Simple Tune in G

This one-handed tune demonstrates the "shrink to fit" principle in action. Notice the similarity between the first and second halves here, and take a minute to play through each at its suggested tempo; it's less complicated than it looks. Watch for the changes from treble to bass clef.

Chapter Ten

10

Left-Hand Accompaniment

In this chapter, we will look at an arrangement that features a quarter-note left-hand pattern which plays the root of the chord then fills out the voicing with the third and seventh. This is a modified version of what is known as a *stride accompaniment* figure. Try to figure out the theory behind the voicings—it will help you to read the left hand more easily.

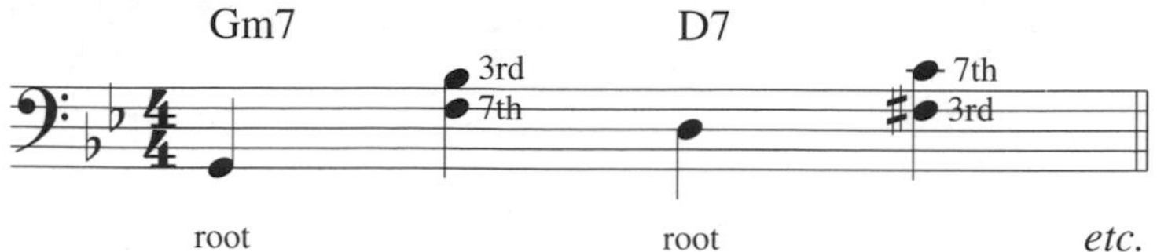

Rhythm Study

Let's try some more sixteenth-note rhythms to help prepare us for the tune.

Note Study

Now let's read through the right and left hand parts as a note study.

Ballad in G Minor

Try this with each hand separately, then both hands together.

Chapter Eleven

11

More Sixteenth Notes

In this chapter, we will work with an arrangement that stretches our knowledge of sixteenth notes and syncopation, incorporating both into a 3/4 time signature. The difference between syncopation in 3/4 time and syncopation in 4/4 is that we cannot see a dividing line down the middle of the measure in 3/4 time. Sometimes the syncopation happens between beats 1 and 2, and sometimes it comes between beats 2 and 3.

Rhythm Study

First let's work out the rhythms.

11

Note Study

Rock Ballad in D

Chapter Twelve

12

Road Map Review

In Chapters 4–8, we looked at symbols and instructions like repeat signs, multiple endings, codas, etc., which tell us to repeat certain sections of music, to skip to a previous section, to skip to an entirely new section, or to finish a piece of music. These symbols and terms form what is sometimes called the musical *road map*—because they guide us through a piece of music much like an actual road map guides us through unfamiliar territory:

- *Repeat signs* tell us to return to a previous repeat (or to the beginning) earlier in the chart.
- *First and second endings* tell us how many times to repeat a section before we go on.
- *Da Capo (D.C.)* tells us to return to the beginning of the chart and play to the end *(Fine),* or some other road map instruction.
- *Dal Segno (D.S.)* tells us to return to the *Sign* (𝄋) and play until the end or another instruction.
- Both D.C. or D.S. can be used in conjunction with a *To Coda* (𝄌) indication, which connects to a final section by means of the coda symbol (𝄌).

These road map instructions are every bit as crucial as the notes and rhythms of a piece of music, and they should be the first thing you look for when approaching a tune for the first time. As a review, without actually playing the notes, see if you can follow the road map of this chart:

In this chapter, we will be looking at a waltz selection. First, we should scope out the road map. No problem there—it's just one time through. However, if we were approaching this as a jazz standard arrangement, we would D.C. for solos and return one more time to the melody after all the solos were done.

Rhythm Study

Look at the rhythm of the right hand first. It's off to an easy start, so you can get comfortable until measure 7. Here, we get some eighth-note syncopation on beats 2 and 3. Now check out measure 10. A dotted eighth-sixteenth rhythm would be articulated "1-uh." The same goes for measure 12 on beat 3. There isn't an exercise for the left hand here; it's just "1, 2," so it should be automatic.

Note Study

Now look at the notes. The right hand moves by leaps of perfect and diminished fifths, then scalewise in a down-up pattern. Try to recognize the pattern; it will help when you are playing both hands. The left hand has the most notes outside the diatonic F scale—play this part slowly until you get the hang of it.

Jazz Waltz in F

Now put the rhythms with the notes, and away you go.

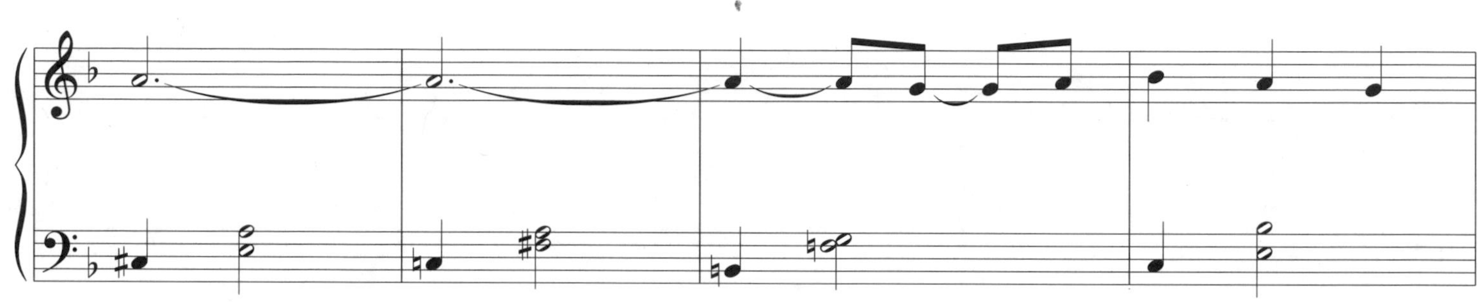

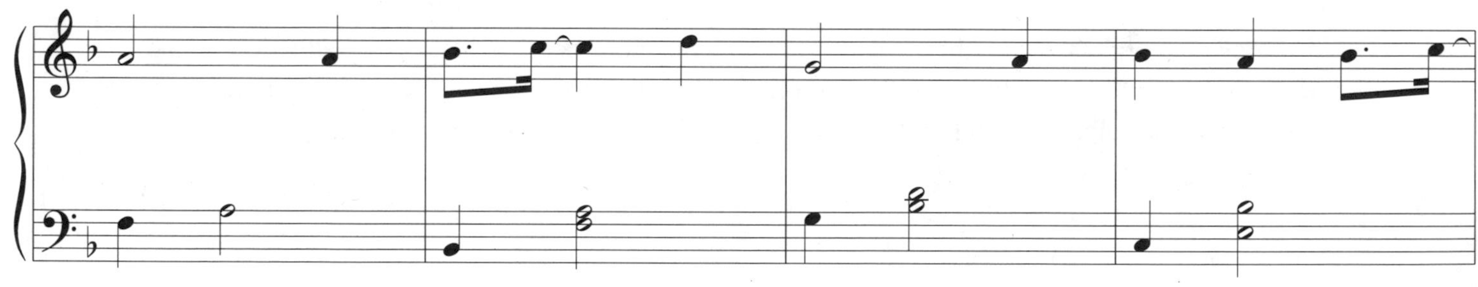

Chapter Thirteen

13

Triplets and Swing

In this chapter, we're going to have some fun with the blues. One part will be the chordal treatment; the other part will be the melody. First, though, we need to look at the basic rhythmic feel of the blues, which is typically described as a *swing,* or *shuffle,* feel.

Swing is based on the idea of the *triplet.* Triplets are any group of three notes that occupy the time equivalent of two of the same kind of note. We already know, for instance, that a quarter note divided into two equal parts is represented as two eighth notes. A quarter note divided into three equal parts is notated as an *eighth-note triplet:*

To practice feeling the rhythm of the eighth-note triplet, tap your foot steadily on the quarter-note pulse and say the word "tri-pl-et," in three syllables, on each tap. If you are stretching the word evenly between each beat, each syllable will fall on an eighth note.

Swing, or shuffle, rhythm can be derived from a triplet rhythm by combining the first two eighth notes of the triplet into a quarter. The result is like a triplet with a silent middle eighth note:

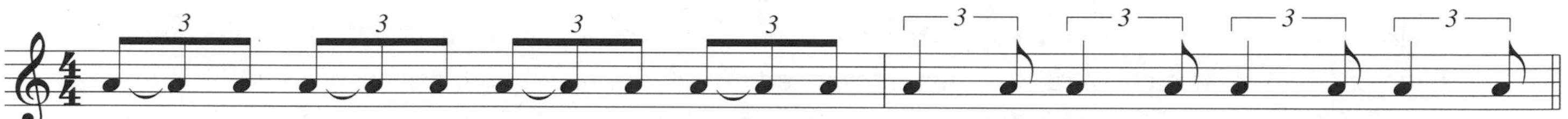

When seen on chord charts, the swing feel is usually notated either by writing the word "swing" above the staff, or by using a notation showing that normal eighth notes should be interpreted with a swing feel (♫ = ♩♪ triplet). This saves the trouble and visual confusion of writing triplet rhythms throughout the piece. As far as the rhythm is concerned, when playing a piece written in straight eighths but with a swing indication, play each eighth-note pair as if it were a quarter note followed by an eighth note within an eighth-note triplet grouping:

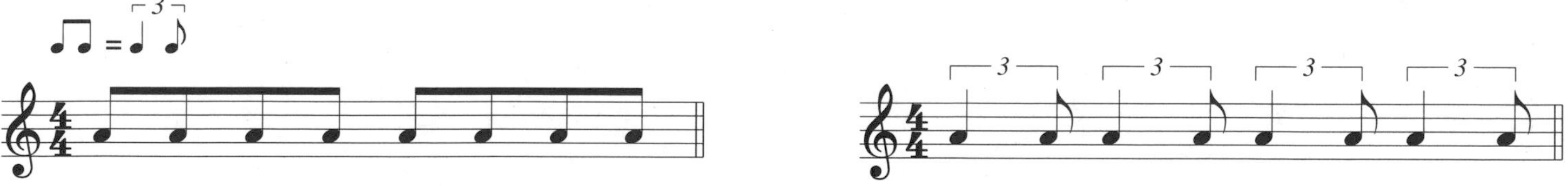

When counting syllables in this situation, use "1-and, 2-and, 3-and," etc.

Rhythm Study

Let's look at the rhythm of the two melodies. Syllables would generally be "1-and, 2-and, 3-and, 4-and" but articulated with a swing, or quarter-eighth, feel. The measures to concentrate on here would be measures 8–10 of the second melody. Syllables for this section would be "1-and, 2-and, and, and, 2-and, and, 2-and, 4-and."

Note Study

Now check out the note study. Thirds move up and back in measures 1–2. The same type of movement occurs in measures 3–4, just transposed. There's a new transposition of an old pattern in measures 7–8, and measure 13 has the final movement. Now look at the left-hand pattern. Remember the scale-step sequence 1–3–5–6–♭7–6–5–3. It transposes to new keys in measures 3–7. Now try the treble clef melodies. There are plenty of half-step approaches to target notes. Look for patterns wherever you can. Keep an eye out for accidentals.

Twelve-Bar Blues in C

This is an arrangement for two players: one on the progression below, and the other on the two melodies, which should be played in alternating fashion. If you don't have a partner, try recording yourself playing the progression, then solo on top of that—or just play the left hand of the progression alone, and use your right hand to play the melodies.

Melody 1

Melody 2

14 Chapter Fourteen

In this chapter, we will look at a tune that displays rhythmic complexity but melodic predictability. It should be played with a very restful, flowing feel.

Rhythm Study

First take a look at the rhythm. The smallest unit is the eighth note. The right hand has relatively few syncopations compared to the left hand, which has several examples of syncopation tied to syncopation. The basic pattern of the left hand is "1-and, and, and, and."

Note Study

Take a look now at the notes. The right hand has a pattern of single notes followed by a fifth, sixth, then a final fifth. There are variations in measures 8–9, but latch on to patterns whenever you can. The left hand is comprised of single notes that look like roots and fifths. There is also some triadic movement.

Pop Ballad in G

Now play one hand at a time with notes and rhythm together. Finally play both hands together. Remember to keep the tempo steady. Don't stop for mistakes; you can correct them after your first reading.

Chapter Fifteen

15

In this chapter, we will look at a tune that is challenging in its use of different time signatures. The basic meter is 3/4, but this alternates with 4/4 in the second half of the tune.

Rhythm Study

Try the right hand first. Keep a steady tempo, and pay close attention to the time changes. Notice the swing indication (♫ = ♩ ♪ triplet). The syllables in measures 15-16 are "1, 3, 1, and." The other measures shouldn't be a big problem, but say the syllables as we have before.

Note Study

Now check out the note exercise. We are in the key of C, so you don't have to keep any flats or sharps in your mind. Take a look at the accidentals though. Measures 13 and 20 of the right hand and measures 1–2, 5, 7–8, 10, and 14–16 of the left hand all have some sort of action in the accidental department.

Jazz Waltz in C

First try each hand alone in a slow but challenging tempo. Then put both hands together at a speed you can accomplish without mistakes. As you become more comfortable with playing this tune, increase the tempo.

Chapter Sixteen

16

In this chapter, we will look at a tune in 3/4 time. The challenge will be in coordinating the left and right hands.

Rhythm Study

First, let's look at the rhythm exercise. Notice that both hands are notated together. Start by working the left and right hands separately, then try them both at once. It's very simple until measures 15 and 16. You may want to concentrate on those.

Note Study

The note exercise involves a key signature of three sharps—the key of A major. Watch out for chords that move in parallel motion, sometimes in a different direction than the left hand. Since they are parallel, however, you can grab the first one and just slide up or down without having to rethink each chord.

Rock Waltz in A

As always, try each hand separately at a challenging tempo, then try them together at a slower tempo until you feel comfortable speeding things up.

Chapter Seventeen

17

The Five Steps to Sightreading

As you've hopefully noticed by now, there are five essential steps to reading any piece of music. The temptation may be to try to read a tune without breaking it down into its component parts—you might think this would save time—but it usually results in many mistakes. To review, here are the steps you should take before reading any new piece of music:

- Check the road map (repeat signs, multiple endings, D.C.s, D.S.s, codas, etc.).
- Find complicated rhythm passages, and use syllables to work them out.
- Check the key signature, and read each note without the rhythm. (Play each note as a quarter note at a steady tempo.)
- Play the notes and rhythms together, but one hand at a time. The tempo should be challenging, but not so fast that you make mistakes.
- Play both hands together at a slower tempo.

Let's apply these steps to our tune this chapter.

First, we should look at the road map. There are repeat signs after the first ending, then the piece reads to the end. This song being a jazz tune, we would probably make an imaginary D.C. for solos, then play the head again to end.

Rhythm Study

Second, we should look at the rhythm. Things get crazy around measure 11 of the tune—syncopations abound here—so let's zero in on those rhythms:

Note Study

Third, we look at the notes alone. For this, we imagine that each note is a quarter note with no rests in between. Give yourself a count-off, and be sure to keep a steady tempo. The tempo does not have to be fast, but it should be consistent; don't slow down or speed up. Here's the right hand—you might also create a note study for the left hand as well.

Swing Tune in F

Now let's give the tune a try with notes and rhythm together—first the right hand, then the left, then both hands together. Good luck!

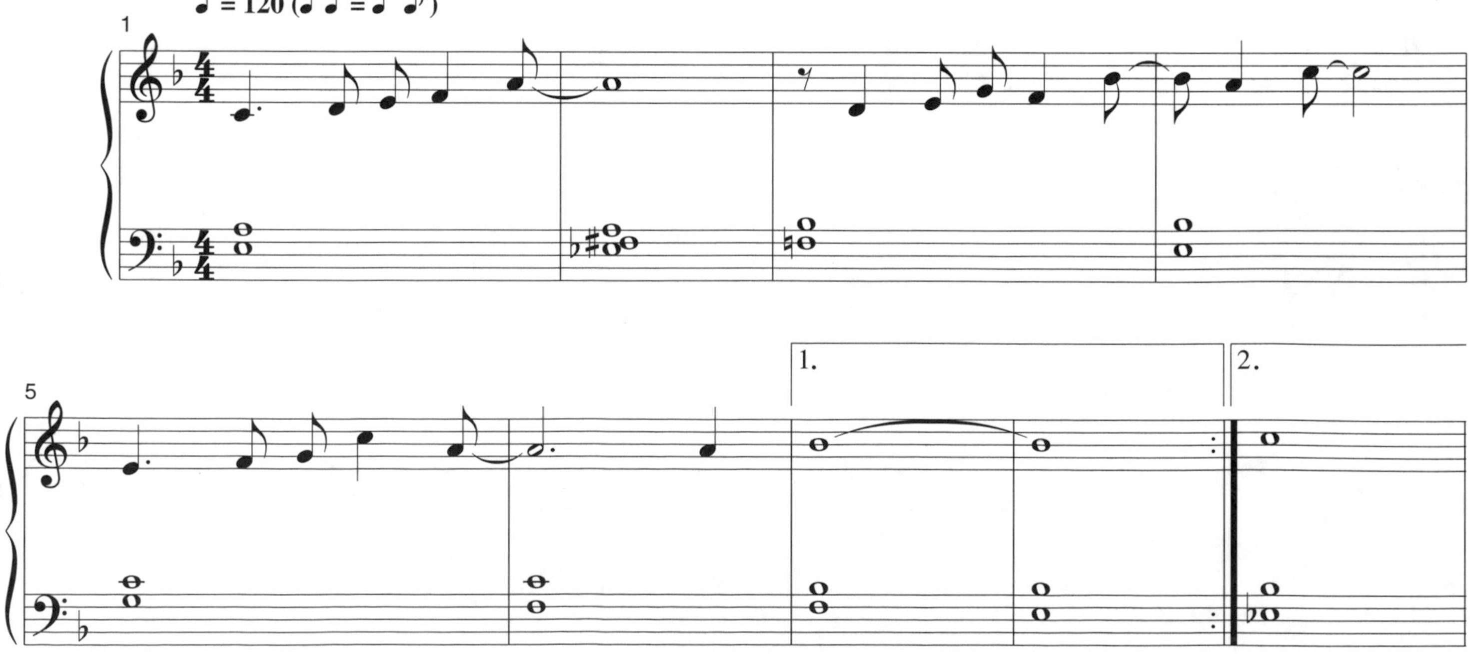

10

14

19

23
To Coda
D.C. al Coda

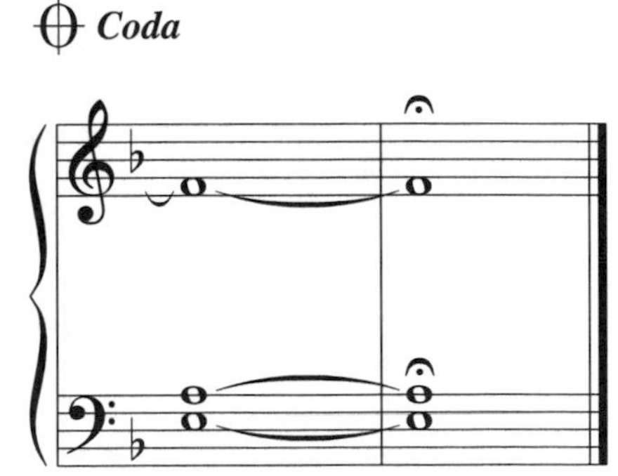
Coda

Chapter Eighteen

18

Dynamic Markings

Our tune in this chapter makes explicit use of dynamics. *Dynamics* are fluctuations in intensity or loudness that add depth, drama, and interest to a tune. They are generally indicated beneath the staff, slightly before the note or notes affected. These are some of the most common dynamic markings:

pp (pianissimo)	very soft	*crescendo*—increase volume gradually
p (piano)	soft	
mp (mezzo piano)	moderately soft	
mf (mezzo forte)	moderately loud	*decrescendo*—decrease volume gradually
f (forte)	loud	
ff (fortissimo)	very loud	

Following the five steps outlined in the previous chapter, let's take a look at our next tune. Our first step should be the road map. This one is pretty simple: there are repeat signs at measures 5 and 12. Measure 20 contains fermatas over the final notes, which tell us to hold these notes indefinitely.

Rhythm Study

Step two would be to examine the rhythm. The left hand should be no problem, so look at the right hand. Let's pick a few measures to work on the syllables. Measure 1 below would be "1-and, and, 3, and." Measure 5 would be "1-uh, 2-and, and, 4-and."

Note Study

Step three would be to play the notes as if they were all quarter notes at a reasonable tempo. Again, the left hand should be fairly simple, so let's focus on the right hand.

Rock Tune in C Minor

Finally, play the notes and rhythms together—first, one hand at a time, then both hands together. Don't forget the dynamic markings. Be sure to start *mezzo forte,* so that you have dynamic room to go to *forte* and back again. My last piece of advice would be that you set your tempo so that it is challenging, but not so fast that you make a lot of mistakes. OK, give it a try.

5
mf
f
mf
9
mf
f
12
mf
mf
f
15
mf
18
f
mf

19 Chapter Nineteen

First, let's look at the road map. It's pretty simple. There are repeats between measures 1 and 26. The vamp from measures 27–30 indicates that we should keep playing until a cue is given.

Rhythm Study

Next, we look at the rhythm alone, for the right hand. You may clap these rhythms or just play them on a single note.

Note Study

Now let's go through the note placement, imagining each note as a quarter note, with no rests. Here's the right hand.

R&B Tune in F

15
18
21
24
D.S.
27
Vamp till cue

Chapter 19

Chapter Twenty

20

You know the drill. Look at the road map first. Take the first ending, and repeat from measure 1, then take the second ending, and play through to the end, where you find a D.S. indication. Go back to the sign (𝄋), and this time take the second ending. Play through to the Fine indication.

Rhythm Study

Let's focus on the right-hand rhythms in measures 9–12 and 16–23 of the tune. Notice the swing indication.

Note Study

Now comes the note recognition. Take it at a reasonable tempo, but don't speed up or slow down. Here's the right hand; try the left hand on your own.

Swing Tune in C Minor

Here comes the final part: putting it all together. Have a good time!

21 Chapter Twenty-One

In this chapter, we will be looking at a rather simple piece. This will leave ample room for an interpretive, emotional reading.

First, take a look at the form. Play through to measure 30, then take the D.C. al Coda. The coda sign is at measure 28. Notice the fermatas in measures 33–35. Time them with great feeling.

Rhythm Study

For the rhythm drill, let's try playing both hands at once. You can't clap this one.

Note Study

For the note recognition, let's look at both the treble and bass clefs separately.

3/4 Ballad in B♭

Here's the tune in its entirety.

22 Chapter Twenty-Two

The Quarter-Note Triplet

In previous chapters, we have worked on tunes written in straight eighths but performed in a "swing" style, playing the eighth-note pairs as if they were a quarter and an eighth in an eighth-note triplet grouping:

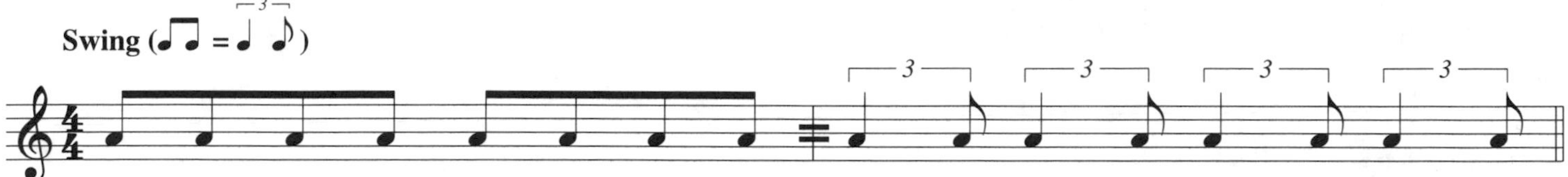

The next level of triplet proficiency is the *quarter-note triplet.* We can derive the quarter-note triplet from the eighth-note triplet. We know the syllables for eighth-note triplets are "1-pl-et, 2-pl-et, 3-pl-et, 4-pl-et," etc. If we tie together the first two eighth notes of this pattern, then the next two, and the next two, we get the syllables for the quarter-note triplet: "1-et-pl, 3-et-pl."

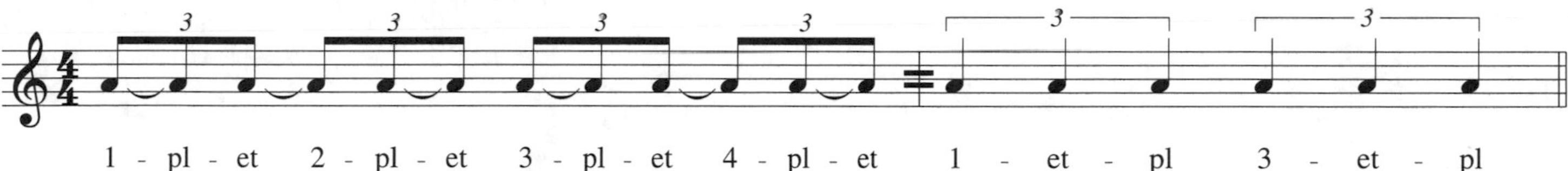

In this chapter, we'll look at a bebop tune—played with a swing feel—which contains some quarter-note triplets. It is arranged for two players—one player on the top treble staff, the other on the grand staff below. We'll focus on the top treble staff in our rhythm and note studies, but I encourage you to study the lower part on your own.

Rhythm Study

Observe the swing indication. This tune should be counted with straight-eighth syllables ("1-and") but with a "quarter-eighth" triplet feel. Don't lose this swing feel in measures 5 and 9 either—those sixteenth notes should be squeezed into the same space as a swung eighth. For the quarter-note triplets, feel each eighth-note triplet, and use the counting method described above.

Note Study

Here are the notes of the top melody.

Bebop Tune in D Minor

4
8
12
3
3
16

To Coda
D.S. al Coda
Coda

Chapter 22

Chapter Twenty-Three

23

Straight Eighths and Triplets

In his chapter, we have another tune arranged for two or three players. This one presents a rhythmic challenge in that it changes from straight eighths to eighth-note triplets and back again—and even includes some quarter-note triplets. Let's try some exercises that work on this principle.

Rhythm Study

Pop Ballad in B♭

Here's the tune. Pick your favorite part to play, and create a note study for it. Then put the notes and rhythms together, and enjoy.

5
9
13
17

21
1.
2.
26
30
35

39
3
3
3
3
3
43
47
3
3
3
3
51

Chapter Twenty-Four

24

In this chapter, we'll be working on a solo piece in 3/4 time. The road map should be no problem; it's just one time through, with no first and second endings or codas. The rhythm is also simple, except for the coordination of the left and right hands. Keep the tempo slow and easy. Pay particular attention to the tempo changes in measures 13, 15, 42, 43, and 55. Read this one with gentle emotion.

Note Study

The biggest challenge is the preponderance of accidentals. The tune goes through many quick key centers, but does not stay long enough in any one to institute a new key signature. This note study will give you an idea of how to handle the notes of the inner voices. Sometimes it is better to grab them with the left hand and sometimes with the right.

3/4 Ballad in C

A Tempo
rit.
rit.

Chapter Twenty-Five

25

12/8 Meter

In this chapter, we will be looking at a piece with a time signature of 12/8. You can think of 12/8 as 4/4 time but with eighth-note triplets as the main beat unit. While we could number each eighth note from one to twelve, let's keep the triplet syllables instead: "1-pl-et, 2-pl-et, 3-pl-et, 4-pl-et." The main thing to remember is that the basic unit is the dotted quarter note, which means that the eighth notes are grouped in threes and feel just like triplets.

Here are some exercises to work this principle.

Rhythm Study

Note Study

Latin Tune in E Minor

7

10

14

17

19

Chapter Twenty-Six

26

Left-Hand Patterns and More Swing Eighths

In this chapter, we will work with swing-eighth rhythm and a repeating boogie-woogie left-hand pattern. Try to figure out, by scale step, what the left-hand pattern of this tune is, and then you won't have to worry about reading each and every note in the bass clef. Just keep up with the chord progression, and plug in the pattern.

Rhythm Study

We'll look at some rhythm examples first. These are not specifically derived from the tune, but they're good practice in playing in a swing feel. Notice, in particular, the "eighth-quarter" triplet figure in some of the measures below—this is the reverse of the typical "quarter-eighth" swing figure but is based on the same underlying triplet feel.

Chapter 26

Note Study

Here's a note study for the left hand. Create one for the right hand on your own.

Boogie-Woogie Tune in F

5
8
11
Fine
14
17
D.S. al Fine

Chapter Twenty-Seven

27

6/8 Meter and Swing Sixteenths

The time signature in this chapter's tune is 6/8. As it has a swing feel (♪♬ = ♩♪ triplet), count the eighth notes "1, 2, 3, 4, 5, 6," inserting "and" for any swung sixteenths off the beat. The one complete sixteenth-note triplet should be counted "6-ta-ta."

Rhythm Study

This rhythm study coordinates left and right hands.

Note Study

Jazz Tune in C Minor

♩. = 120 (♫ = ♩♪ triplet)

1

6

10

28 Chapter Twenty-Eight

In this chapter we will play a beautiful ballad. First take a look at the road map: no problem there, just one time through.

Rhythm Study

Next, let's look at this rhythm study. We'll focus on the right hand, as the left hand in this piece is relatively easy. The first couple of measures here shouldn't give you a lot of trouble—use this time to get comfortable before the difficult parts begins. Measure 3 has some syncopation in beat 3 tied to a triplet on beat 4. The syllables of the triplet are "(silent 4)-pl-et." The next measure to concentrate on is measure 7 with its dotted eighth-sixteenth pattern. Measure 12 also has sixteenth-note activity. The next new piece of information might be measure 21, which is just a variation of measure 3. Syllables for that measure would be "1, e, pl-et."

28

Note Study

Now let's move on to the note study. Watch out for the key signature—most of the problems occur when we step outside of the key for a moment. Look first at measure 7. Figure out the bottom note on beat 2, and notice that the B♭ from beat 1 moves to a B♮. Now check out the chord on beat 2 of measure 9. It is, from top to bottom, G♯, E, and D♯. Except for the F triad, we stay with sharps until measure 12, where we return to flats on beat 2. Measure 14 begins with both an E♭ and an F♯ in the chord. Everything else looks pretty readable. Just take your time, and keep a steady tempo.

9

13

17

21

25

Pop Ballad in B♭

8
12
16
20
3
24

29 Chapter Twenty-Nine

In this chapter, we will look at a swing tune.

Rhythm Study

There's not a lot of challenge in the rhythm department, but let's talk about it. The basic feel is a swing-eighth groove. We've got a repeating pattern in measures 1, 3, 7, 17, 19, 23, and 35. We see our old friend syncopation in measures 5 and 21. The only other measures to look at are measure 25 and 27 with their sixteenth notes. Syllables would be "1-and, and-uh, 3, 4-and"—remember that "and-uh" actually fits in the same amount of time as "and" because of the swing feel.

Note Study

The note exercise is also pretty tame. Keep the key signature in mind, because the first four measures are diatonic. Around measure 5, we get more accidentals. There is a general pattern that is set up in measure 1, which is "four notes descending, with a leap down between notes 2 and 3." Try to figure out the chord in the left hand by analyzing two-beat chunks.

Chapter 29

Swing Tune in E♭

Try each hand separately with notes and rhythms combined, then try them both together. Take a steady tempo, and play without stopping. If you make a mistake, don't try to correct it while you're reading—come back to it later.

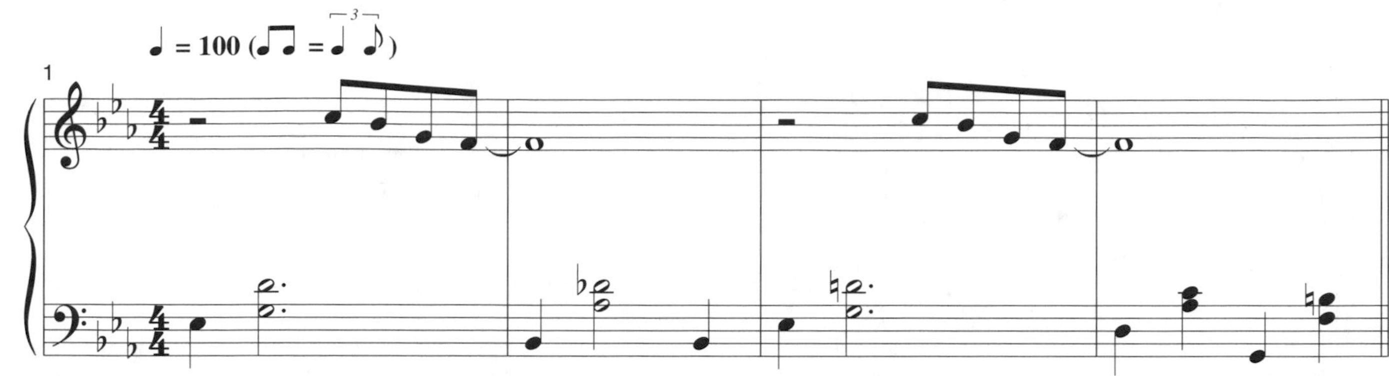

17
21
25
29
34

30 Chapter Thirty

In this chapter, we will look at a song with a challenging left-hand/right-hand coordination. I hope you enjoy learning it.

Rhythm Study

Let's start with the rhythm. Syncopations are found in measures 1–2, 5–6, and 16–19; they're everywhere, but nothing we haven't seen before. Check out the sixteenth-note triplets in measure 10. We'll see this rhythm several more times. Now focus on the meter change in measure 37. We have a time signature of 5/4, or five quarter notes per measure. Syllables here would be "1, 2, and, and," and then, in measure 40, "1, 2, 4-and, 5-and." Now switch back to 4/4 time.

Note Study

Take a look at the note exercise; it goes on for quite a while. Keep the key signature in mind, and concentrate on the chords in the treble clef. Next, play through the bass clef at a reasonable tempo.

24
29
34
39
1
6
11
16
21
26

Latin Tune in G

The tempo for this tune is moderate, but find a tempo at which you can keep up, without having to slow down or stop to fix a wrong note.

33
37
41
45
49
To Coda
D.S. al Coda
Coda
53
1., 2., 3.
4.

Chapter Thirty-One

In this chapter, we will look at another swing jazz tune. The main challenge will be to deal with the time signature of 5/4.

Rhythm Study

Take a look at the rhythm exercise first. The first measure starts on beat 4. Measure each rest and note with the basic number of quarter notes equaling five. Sixteenth triplets have syllables of 1-ta-ta,and-ta-ta, so measure 3 goes something like, "1, 4, and-ta-ta, 5." The other measures shouldn't be too hard as they are comprised mainly of eighth notes. Just keep the five-beat grouping in mind, and everything will be fine.

Note Study

Now check out the note exercise. Our key signature could be problematic—six flats! Look at the signature, and glue it in your mind. The accidentals in this piece are few, but check out the B♭♭s, as well as the C♮s. Keep a steady tempo, and don't stop.

5/4 Jazz Tune in E♭ Minor

Now try each hand alone with notes and rhythm, then both hands together at a slow but steady tempo.

14
17
20
3
23
3
26
3
3

Chapter Thirty-Two

In this chapter, we will look at a very syncopated ballad. There are many challenges in this tune, both in the rhythms and the notes.

Rhythm Study

Looking at rhythm first, you'll see that syncopations are all over the place. Be sure to articulate the syllables ("1-ee-and-uh"), or a variation of those, in order to figure out the tied rhythms. Some notable sixteenth-note syncopation occurs in measures 1–3, 7, 11, 32, and 39. Another challenge involves the triplets in measures 4 and 28. Try to perform them as evenly as possible.

Note Study

Now check out the notes. Keep the key signature firmly in mind: E major (four sharps). Things get more complex in measures 15–18. Here you will find many accidentals as the key seems to be changing rapidly. It would not do any good to change key signatures here because the keys do not last long enough. Measures 21–23 seem to be in the key of C major, and, except for a few chromatic approach notes, that key remains until measure 31. Check out the new key in measure 35; it is A major, but again the key quickly disintegrates in measures 45 and 46. Be sure to run through the notes in the left hand as well.

Chapter 32

Pop Ballad in E

As usual, try each hand alone incorporating rhythm and notes. Keep a steady tempo while putting the hands together. This tune is a ballad, so the tempo should not be fast—about 50 bpm should do it. Have a great time reading this one.

19
1.
22
28
2.
33
37

The Best in Music Instruction from Hal Leonard

Musicians Institute Press is the official series of Southern California's renowned music school, Musicians Institute. MI instructors, some of the finest musicians in the world, share their vast knowledge and experience for all levels of students in this series of books. For guitar, bass, drums, vocals, and keyboards, MI Press offers the finest music curriculum for higher learning through a variety of series:

- ***Essential Concepts*** – designed from MI core curriculum programs
- ***Master Class*** – designed from MI elective courses
- ***Private Lessons*** – tackle a variety of topics "one-on-one" with MI faculty instructors
- ***Workshop Series*** – transcribed scores, designed from MI's performance workshop classes

ADVANCED SCALE CONCEPTS & LICKS FOR GUITAR

by Jean Marc Belkadi
Private Lessons
The complete resource for applying pentatonic, harmonic minor, melodic minor, whole tone, and diminished scales. The CD includes 99 full-band tracks.
______00695298 Book/CD Pack..................$12.95

BASIC BLUES GUITAR

by Steve Trovato
Private Lessons
Play rhythm guitar in the style of Stevie Ray Vaughan, B.B. King, Chuck Berry, T-Bone Walker, Albert King, Freddie Green, and many more! CD includes 40 full-demo tracks and the instruction covers all styles of blues and the essential chords, patterns and riffs.
______00695180 Book/CD Pack..................$12.95

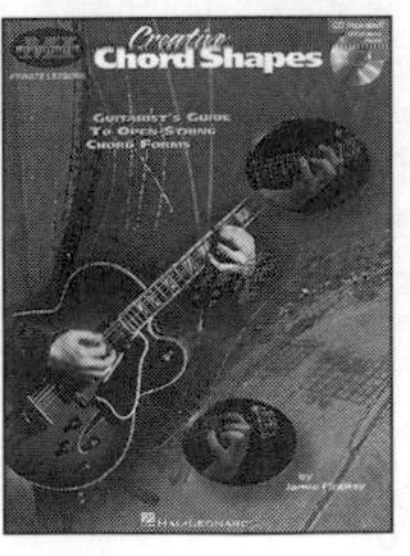

CREATIVE CHORD SHAPES

Guitarist's Guide to Open-String Chord Forms
by Jamie Findlay
Private Lessons
This book/CD pack lets guitarists explore the lush sounds of open-string chords. The CD includes 19 full-demo examples covering: arpeggiated progressions, arpeggiated chords and scalar lines, adding open strings to diatonic chords, and more.
______00695172 Book/CD Pack....................$7.95

THE DIMINISHED SCALE FOR GUITAR

by Jean Marc Belkadi
Private Lessons
Jean Marc Belkadi reveals the secrets of using the diminished scale in over 30 lessons and sample phrases. The CD includes over 30 tracks for demonstration and play-along.
______00695227 Book/CD Pack....................$9.95

GUITAR BASICS

Essential Chords, Scales, Rhythms, and Theory
by Bruce Buckingham
Private Lessons
This pack gives essential instruction on open chords, barre chords, power chords, strumming; scales, rhythm playing, the blues, and moveable chord shapes. It includes inversions, "color" chords, practice tips, chord charts, songs, and progressions.
______00695134 Book/CD Pack..................$14.95

GUITAR HANON

by Peter Deneff
Private Lessons
51 exercises for the beginning to professional guitarist, covering: diatonic, chromatic, major, minor, dominant, and half-diminished seventh arpeggios, whole tone exercises, diminished arpeggios, and more.
______00695321..$9.95

GUITAR SOLOING

The Contemporary Guide to Improvisation
by Daniel Gilbert and Beth Marlis
Essential Concepts
A comprehensive source for mastering the art of single note, melodic improvisation. The CD includes over 30 tracks for demonstration and play-along. The topics covered include: scales, modes, arpeggios, technique and visualization exercises; rock, blues, jazz, and other styles; and sequences, phrases, and licks.
______00695190 Book/CD Pack..................$17.95

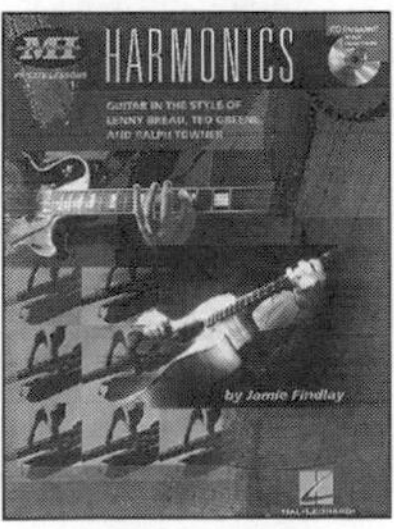

HARMONICS

Guitar in the Style of Lenny Breau, Ted Greene, and Ralph Towner
by Jamie Findlay
Private Lessons
This pack covers: harp harmonics and natural harmonics; combining harmonics with hammers and pulls; and more. The CD includes 30 full-demo examples.
______00695169 Book/CD Pack....................$9.95

JAZZ GUITAR CHORD SYSTEM

by Scott Henderson
Private Lessons
The essential guide to jazz chord voicings and substitutions, complete with a color-coded method for over 500 essential voicings. Players will understand chord functions and their harmonic possibilities better than ever before, as well as inversions, extensions, alterations, and substitutions. Players will also be able to increase their harmonic vocabulary for accompaniment, composing and chord-melody playing.
______00695291..$6.95

JAZZ GUITAR IMPROVISATION

by Sid Jacobs
Master Class
Develop your solo skills with this comprehensive method which includes a CD with 99 full demonstration tracks. Topics include: common jazz phrases; applying scales and arpeggios; guide tones, non-chordal tones, fourths; and more.
______00695128 Book/CD Pack..................$17.95

MODERN APPROACH TO JAZZ, ROCK & FUSION GUITAR

by Jean Marc Belkadi
Private Lessons
Over 30 great lines using a variety of techniques and melodic ideas. Covers: alternate, sweep, and skip picking; major scale, chromaticism, arpeggios, superimposing triads; legato, wide intervals, alterations; and much more. Includes standard notation and tablature.
______00695143 Book/CD Pack..................$12.95

MUSIC READING FOR GUITAR

The Complete Method
by David Oakes
Essential Concepts
The ultimate guide to music reading, with over 450 songs and examples. Covers these topics: notes, rhythms, keys, positions, dynamics, syncopation, chord charts, duets, scale forms, phrasing, odd time, and much more!
______00695192..$16.95

RHYTHM GUITAR – THE COMPLETE GUIDE

by Bruce Buckingham & Eric Paschal
Essential Concepts

A comprehensive source for learning rhythm guitar in a variety of musical styles. It covers: open chords, barre chords, and other movable shapes; strumming, fingerstyle, flatpicking and arpeggiation; common progressions and basic chord theory; triads, sixth, seventh, ninth, and many other chords; and much more.

_______00695188..$16.95

ROCK LEAD BASICS

by Nick Nolan and Danny Gill
Master Class

A method exploring the techniques, scales and fundamentals used by the greatest legends of rock guitar. CD includes over 75 full demonstration tracks. Covers pentatonic and diatonic scales, bending, vibrato, lead licks, and more. Includes standard notation and tab.

_______00695144 Book/CD Pack..................$14.95

ROCK LEAD PERFORMANCE

by Nick Nolan and Danny Gill
Master Class

Techniques, scales and soloing concepts for guitar complete with a CD containing over 70 full-demo tracks; in-depth study of modes; soloing over chord changes and modulations; harmonic minor, diminished and other scales; blues-based music; and much more!

_______00695278 Book/CD Pack..................$16.95

ROCK LEAD TECHNIQUES

by Nick Nolan and Danny Gill
Master Class

Licks, scales, and soloing concepts for guitar, including: picking technique, three-note-per-string scales, sweep picking, fingerpicking, and string skipping, solo constructions, harmonics, and more. CD includes 97 full demo tracks.

_______00695146 Book/CD Pack..................$14.95

BASS

ARPEGGIOS FOR BASS

by David Keif
Private Lessons

The ultimate reference guide for electric bass! This book covers triad and seventh chord arpeggios, patterns covering the entire 4-string neck, easy-to-use fretboard diagrams, inversions, and more.

_______00695133..$12.95

BASS FRETBOARD BASICS

by Paul Farnen
Essential Concepts

All you need to know about the bass fretboard, including: scales, intervals, triads, modal patterns, and fundamentals; keys, fingerings, position playing; arpeggios, turnarounds, walking bass lines; horizontal and vertical playing; for all styles of playing!

_______00695201..$12.95

BASS PLAYING TECHNIQUES

by Alexis Sklarevski
Essential Concepts

A comprehensive source for playing bass in a variety of musical styles. Explains: hammer-ons, pull-offs, bends, muting, vibrato; slap bass grooves; essential bass lines and basic theory; exercises, picking suggestions, sample songs; and more!

_______00695207..$14.95

GROOVES FOR ELECTRIC BASS

by David Keif
Private Lessons

Grooving – the marriage of the rhythmic feel to the harmony – should be an integral part of a bassist's practice routine, and author David Keif provides a variety of grooves that will help develop any player's skills. This book provides essential patterns and bass lines for rock, pop, blues, funk, R&B, jazz, hip-hop, and other styles. The CD includes 36 tracks for demonstration and play-along.

_______00695265 Book/CD Package............$12.95

MUSIC READING FOR BASS – THE COMPLETE GUIDE

by Wendi Hrebovcsik
Essential Concepts

A comprehensive source for sight-reading fundamentals, including notes, rhythms, keys, positions, and scale forms. Also teaches reading from chord symbols, following charts, creating walking bass lines, slides, ghost notes, and other techniques.

_______00695203..$9.95

ODD METER BASSICS

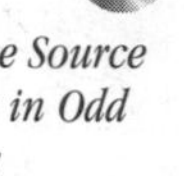

A Comprehensive Source for Playing Bass in Odd Time Signatures
by Dino Monoxelos
Private Lessons

This pack helps bassists play effortlessly in any time signature! Covers: 3/4, 3/8, 6/4, 6/8, 12/8, 5/4, 5/8, 7/4, 7/8, 9/8, 11/8; multiple-meter charts; playing over the bar line; more! The CD includes 49 full-demo tracks.

_______00695170 Book/CD Pack.................$14.95

KEYBOARD

MUSIC READING FOR KEYBOARD

by Larry Steelman
Essential Concepts

A complete method for: notes, rhythms, keys, time signatures; treble and bass clefs; right and left hand patterns and accompaniments; popular song styles; repeat signs, accidentals, codas; and more.

_______00695205..$12.95

R&B SOUL KEYBOARD

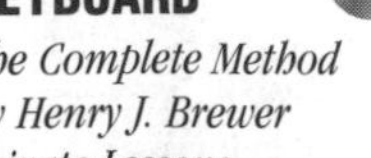

The Complete Method
by Henry J. Brewer
Private Lessons

A hands-on guide to the essential R&B soul grooves, chords, and techniques. It covers Gospel and soul keyboard voicings, technique, independence, and the left hand, rhythm, feel, groove, and much more. The CD includes 99 full-band tracks.

_______00695327 Book/CD Pack.................$16.95

SALSA HANON
50 Essential Exercises for Latin Piano
by Peter Deneff
Private Lessons
50 patterns for the beginning to professional pianist, including the styles of Latin, Cuban, Montuno, Salsa, and Cha-Cha.
_______00695226...$10.95

DRUMS

BRAZILIAN COORDINATION FOR DRUMSET
Private Lessons
by Maria Martinez
In this essential method and workbook, Maria Martinez reveals her revolutionary studies for Brazilian drumset coordination. She covers Bossa Nova, Samba and Baiao Ostinatos, 3/4 Bossa Nova/Samba, 7/4 Bossa Nova/Samba, rhythm studies, and more! The CD includes 48 full band tracks.
_______00695284 Book/CD Pack.................$14.95

CHART READING WORKBOOK FOR DRUMMERS
by Bobby Gabriele
Private Lessons
This book/CD covers common symbols and musical shorthand, section figures and ensemble figures, accents, set-up ideas, and embellishment, and swing, big band, and other styles. The CD includes 16 full-demo examples.
_______00695129 Book/CD Pack.................$14.95

WORKING THE INNER CLOCK FOR DRUMSET
by Phil Maturano
Private Lessons
This book/CD pack is a fun, effective, and innovative tool for improving players' chops. The CD includes 16 complete play-along tracks; the lessons cover rock, Motown, funk, shuffle, calypso, big band, fusion, Latin and other grooves; the book includes complete charts with instructional advice and sample groove and fill ideas as well as tips on improving ensemble reading and technique.
_______00695127 Book/CD Pack.................$16.95

VOICE

SIGHTSINGING
by Mike Campbell
Essential Concepts
Includes over 300 examples and exercises and covers: major, minor, modes and the blues; arpeggios, chromaticism, rhythm and counting; professional lead sheets; and much more!
_______00695195...$16.95

ALL INSTRUMENTS

AN APPROACH TO JAZZ IMPROVISATION
by Dave Pozzi
Private Lessons
This book/CD pack explores the styles of Charlie Parker, Clifford Brown, Sonny Rollins, Bud Powell, and others for a comprehensive guide to jazz improvisation. The CD includes 99 tracks for play-along and demonstration. Topics include: scale choices, chord analysis, phrasing, memorization, transposition of solos, melodies, and harmonic progressions, and much more.
_______00695135 Book/CD Pack.................$17.95

ENCYCLOPEDIA OF READING RHYTHMS
by Gary Hess
Private Lessons
A comprehensive guide to: notes, rests, counting, subdividing, time signatures; triplets, ties, dotted notes and rests; cut time, compound time, swing, shuffle; rhythm studies, counting systems, road maps; and more!
_______00695145...$19.95

GOING PRO
Developing a Professional Career in the Music Industry
by Kenny Kerner
Private Lessons
Everything you need to know to go pro, including information about personal managers, music attorneys, business managers and booking agents, record companies, A&R, publishing, songwriting, demo tapes and press kits, self-promotion, and much more.
_______00695322...$16.95

HARMONY AND THEORY
by Keith Wyatt and Carl Schroeder
Essential Concepts
This book is a step-by-step guide to MI's well-known Harmony and Theory class. It includes complete lessons and analysis of: intervals, rhythms, scales, chords, key signatures; transposition, chord inversions, key centers; harmonizing the major and minor scales; and more!
_______00695161...$17.95

LEAD SHEET BIBLE
by Robin Randall and Janice Peterson
Private Lessons
This book/CD package is for the singer, songwriter, or musician who wants to create a lead sheet or chord chart that is easy to follow. The CD includes over 70 demo tracks. The instruction covers: song form, transposition, considering the instrumentation, scales, keys, rhythm, chords, slash notation, and other basics, and more. It also includes sample songs, common terms, and important tips for anyone putting music on paper!
_______00695130 Book/CD Pack.................$19.95

WORKSHOP SERIES

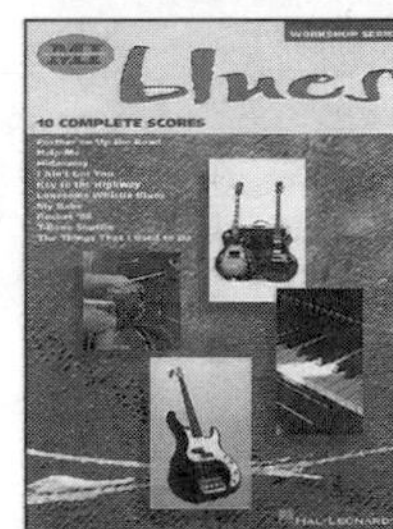

Each of these books includes 10 transcribed scores of music's greatest songs, designed from MI's performance workshop classes. Each part is analyzed to give "behind-the-scenes" understanding of why these songs are classics and how to perform them.

BLUES WORKSHOP
Help Me • Key to the Highway • T-Bone Shuffle • The Things I Used to Do • and more.
_______00695137...$22.95

CLASSIC ROCK
Born to Be Wild • Get Back • Iron Man • Sunshine of Your Love • Walk This Way • and more.
_______00695136...$19.95

R&B WORKSHOP
Ain't No Mountain High Enough • Get Ready • Gimme Some Lovin' • (You Make Me Feel Like) A Natural Woman • Reach Out, I'll Be There • What's Going On • You Keep Me Hangin' On • and more.
_______00695138...$24.95

Guitar Reference, Instruction & Techniques

ADVANCED CONCEPTS AND TECHNIQUES

A Complete Guide To Mastering The Guitar

The perfect follow-up book for graduates of the Wolf Marshall Guitar Method. With this book, you'll explore the advanced styles of today's greatest players from jazz to monster rock dudes and learn how to combine all you know to make music – your music. Chapters include: triads, scale combining, modes, arpeggios, pentatonics, wide intervals, tap-on technique, and more.

_______00697253..$9.95

ALTERNATE TUNINGS FOR GUITAR

by Dave Whitehill

Over 300 tunings from Michael Hedges, Jimmy Page, Sonic Youth, Will Ackerman, Alex de Grassi, Soundgarden, Joni Mitchell, and many more. Includes drop, open, modal, unison, slack, and hybrid tunings.

_______00695217..$4.95

BASIC GUITAR ADJUSTMENTS & SETUPS

by John Boehnlein

An essential guide to guitar maintenance, covering: essential tools and inspection tips; neck, action, intonation, and pickup adjustments; re-stringing; adjusting vibrato bridges; and more.

_______00695149..$4.95

BLUES YOU CAN USE

by John Ganapes

A comprehensive source for learning blues guitar, designed to develop both your lead and rhythm playing. Covers all styles of blues, including Texas, Delta, R&B, early rock and roll, gospel, blues/rock and more. Includes 21 complete solos; blues chords, progressions and riffs; turnarounds; moveable scales and soloing techniques; string bending; audio with leads and full band backing; and more!

_______00695007 Book/CD Pack.................$19.95
_______00695276 Spanish Edition $19.95

ELECTRIC SLIDE GUITAR METHOD

by David Hamburger

This book/CD pack is a comprehensive examination of slide guitar fundamentals. You get lessons on the styles of Duane Allman, Dave Hole, Ry Cooder, Bonnie Raitt, Muddy Waters, Johnny Winter, and Elmore James. Also includes: sample licks and solos; info on selecting a slide and proper setup; backup/rhythm slide playing; standard and open tunings; and more.

_______00695022 Book/CD Pack...................$19.95

***FAST*TRACK GUITAR CHORDS & SCALES**

Over 1,400 chords, essential scale and mode patterns, including pentatonic, diatonic, harmonic minor, melodic minor, and many other scales. PLUS! Unique play-along "jam session" with 20 different chord progressions.

_______00697291 Book/CD Pack.....................$9.95

THE GUITAR F/X COOKBOOK

by Chris Amelar

The ultimate source for guitar tricks, effects, and other unorthodox techniques. This book demonstrates and explains 45 incredible guitar sounds using common stomp boxes and a few unique techniques, including: pick scraping, police siren, ghost slide, church bell, jaw harp, delay swells, looping, monkey's scream, cat's meow, race car, pickup tapping, and much more.

_______00695080 Book/CD Pack...................$14.95

GUITAR LICKS

by Chris Amelar

Learn great licks in the style of players like Clapton, Hendrix, Hammett, Page and more. Includes two complete solos; 40 must-know licks for rock and blues; info on essential techniques; standard notation & tab; and more. CD features demos of every technique, lick and solo in the book.

_______00695141 Book/CD Pack.................$14.95

JAZZ GUITAR CHORD MELODIES

arranged & performed by Dan Towey

This book/CD pack includes complete solo performances of 12 standards, including: All the Things You Are • Body and Soul • My Romance • How Insensitive • My One and Only Love • and more. The arrangements are performance level and range in difficulty from intermediate to advanced.

_______00698988 Book/CD Pack...................$19.95

TERRIFYING TECHNIQUE FOR GUITAR

by Carl Culpepper

The ultimate source for building chops while improving your technical facility and overcoming physical barriers. Covers: alternate, economy, hybrid, and sweep picking; symetrical, chromatic, and scale exercises; arpeggios, tapping, legato, and bending sequences – over 200 exercises in all. CD includes full demonstrations of the exercises.

_______00695034 Book/CD Pack...................$14.95

ULTIMATE EAR TRAINING FOR GUITAR AND BASS

by Gary Willis

Everything you need to improve your ear training, including a CD with 99 full-demo tracks, vital information on intervals, rhythms, melodic shapes, inversions, scales, chords, extensions, alterations, fretboard visualization, and fingering diagrams.

_______00695182 Book/CD Pack.................$12.95

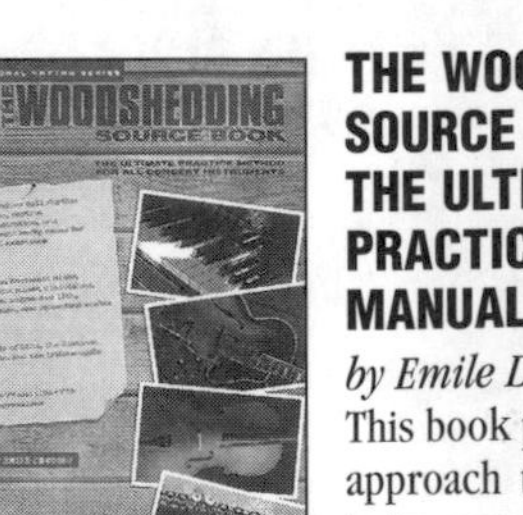

THE WOODSHEDDING SOURCE BOOK – THE ULTIMATE PRACTICE MANUAL

by Emile De Cosmo

This book presents a proven approach to practicing and is, in essence, woodshedding in book form. Rehearsing with this method daily will improve your technique, reading ability, rhythmic and harmonic vocabulary, eye/finger coordination, endurance, range, theoretical knowledge, and listening skills – all which lead to superior improvisational skills. The CD provides full rhythm section and harmonic background for all 66 exercises.

_______00842000 Book/CD Pack...................$19.95

Bass Reference, Instruction & Techniques

BASS IMPROVISATION

The Complete Guide to Soloing
by Ed Friedland

This book/CD pack is designed to help players master the art of improvisation. The CD includes over 50 tracks for demonstration and play-along. The book works with electric or acoustic bass and covers: modes, harmonic minor, melodic minor, blues, pentatonics, diminished, whole tone, Lydian b7, Mixolydian b13, and other important scales; phrasing, chord scale concepts, melodic development, guide tones, and resolutions; plus how to use your ear, practice tunes, and much more!

_______00695164 Book/CD Pack..................$17.95

FUNK BASS

by Jon Liebman

Critically acclaimed as the best single source for the techniques used to play funk and slap-style bass! Includes a foreword by John Patitucci and is endorsed by Rich Appleman of the Berklee College Of Music, Will Lee, Mark Egan, Stuart Hamm and many others! Features several photos and a special section on equipment and effects. A book for everyone – from beginners to advanced players! Includes a 58-minute audio accompaniment.

_______00699347 Book/Cassette Pack..........$14.95
_______00699348 Book/CD Pack..................$17.95

FUNK/ FUSION BASS

by Jon Liebman

This follow-up to Funk Bass studies the techniques and grooves of today's top funk/fusion bass players. It includes sections on mastering the two-finger technique, string crossing, style elements, establishing a groove, building a funk/fusion soloing vocabulary, and a CD with over 90 tracks to jam along with. Features a foreword written by Earth, Wind And Fire bassist Verdine White.

_______00696553 Book/CD Pack..................$19.95

FINGERBOARD HARMONY FOR BASS

A Linear Approach For 4-, 5- and 6-String Bass
by Gary Willis

A comprehensive source for learning the theory and geometry of the bass fingerboard by one of today's leading players and instructors. Audio features Gary Willis demonstrating 99 examples and exercises.

_______00695043 Book/CD Pack..................$17.95

JAZZ BASS

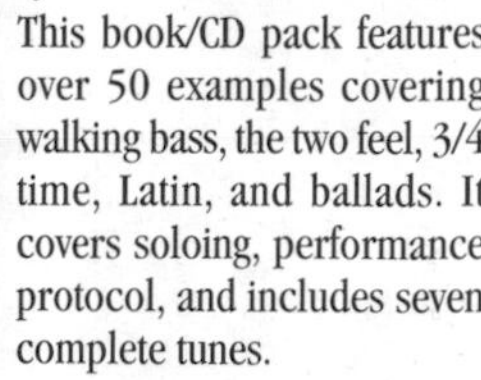

by Ed Friedland

This book/CD pack features over 50 examples covering walking bass, the two feel, 3/4 time, Latin, and ballads. It covers soloing, performance protocol, and includes seven complete tunes.

_______00695084 Book/CD Pack..................$17.95

JUMP 'N' BLUES BASS

by Keith Rosier

Essential jump/swing and modern blues bass lines for electric and upright players. Includes lessons and music in the style of Willie Dixon, Larry Taylor, Edgar Willis, Duck Dunn, Tommy Shannon, and more! The CD includes a lives blues band with over 20 play-along tracks.

_______00695292 Book/CD Pack..................$14.95

LOST ART OF COUNTRY BASS

by Keith Rosier
Endorsed by Leland Sklar & Glenn Worf

An introduction to country bass for electric or upright players. This book/CD pack is an insider's look at country bass playing on stage and in the studio. The book includes lessons and music in the style of Hank Williams, Lefty Frizzel, Marty Stuart, David Ball, and more. The CD includes 35 songs with full band backing. You'll learn classic and modern country bass lines, how to be a studio bassist, how to read music with the Nashville Number System, and more!

"A killer country primer."

– Bass Player magazine

_______00695107 Book/CD Pack..................$17.95

MUTED GROOVES

by Josquin des Pres

Develop the string muting, string raking, and right-hand techniques used by the greatest legends of bass with this comprehensive exercise book. It includes over 100 practical exercises with audio accompaniments for each.

_______00696555 Book/CD Pack..................$16.95

REGGAE BASS

by Ed Friedland

The complete guide to reggae and Jamaican bass styles, covering early ska, rock steady, roots reggae, dub, modern ska, dance hall, and more. The book includes performance tips and lessons, authentic grooves and riddims, and more. The CD includes 47 full-demo tracks.

_______00695163 Book/CD Pack..................$12.95

ROCK BASS

by Jon Liebman

Learn the essential rock grooves and bass lines in the style of Paul McCartney, John Entwistle, John Paul Jones, Geddy Lee, Sting, Billy Sheehan, Flea, and many more! The CD includes 99 full-demo tracks for every exercise in the book and the book itself includes tips on all the essential techniques, grooves and bass lines from the 1950s through the 1990s. Also includes tips on equipment, effects, and listening suggestions.

_______00695083 Book/CD Pack..................$17.95

RON CARTER – BUILDING JAZZ BASS LINES

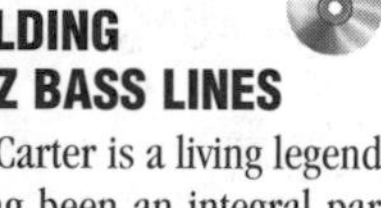

Ron Carter is a living legend, having been an integral part of the Miles Davis group and V.S.O.P. In this book/CD package, Ron shows the student how to create more creative bass lines in a step-by-step process that will yield creative results in a very short time. The exercises in the book (blues in major and minor keys, 3/4 blues), as well as three of Ron's compositions, are performed by an all-star rhythm section of Ron on bass, Mulgrew Miller on piano, Ofer Ganor on guitar, and Lewis Nash on drums. Ron's part can be isolated on each track, so you can listen to him play the exercises, play along with him, and then turn his track off and create your own bass lines with the guitar, piano, and drums.

_______00841240 Book/CD Pack..................$19.95

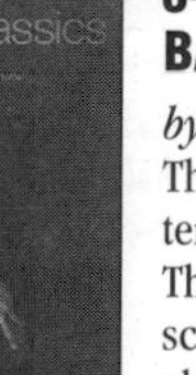

6-STRING BASSICS

by David Gross

The complete guide for mastering the six-string bass. This book/CD pack covers scales, arpeggios, modes, chord forms, two-handed tapping, alternative techniques, chromatic exercises and theory concepts. The CD includes 99 full-demo tracks.

_______00695221 Book/CD Pack..................$12.95

Keyboard Reference, Instruction & Techniques

ASPIRING JAZZ PIANIST

by Debbie Denke

There is no joy like that of expressing yourself through musical improvisation. This book/CD pack will show you how to arrange and improvise to popular and jazz tunes in your own style, using a clear, step-by-step method developed over many years by successful jazz pianist and teacher Debbie Denke. It can be used for personal instruction or as a classroom text. The CD features both solo piano demonstrations and bass and drum accompaniments that let you practice playing with a rhythm section.

_______00290480 Book/CD Pack..................$24.95

BLUES RIFFS FOR PIANO

by Ed Baker
Great Riffs Series
Cherry Lane Music

The definitive source for blues riffs and licks! Features performance notes for and accompanying audio examples of fills and embellishments, turnarounds, tags and licks in the style of Ray Charles, Dr. John, Professor Longhair, and Johnny Johnson.

_______02503615 Book/CD Pack..................$17.95

COUNTRY RIFFS FOR PIANO

by George Wurzbach
Great Riffs Series
Cherry Lane Music

The ultimate source for learning country riffs and licks! Features concise performance notes on how to play more than 25 fills, turnarounds, tags, comping patterns, and solos. Also includes a history of the piano in country music, as well as an accompanying audio cassette or CD of the examples, all in one riff-packed, easy-to-follow book.

_______02503613 Book/CD Pack..................$17.95

DR. JOHN TEACHES NEW ORLEANS PIANO VOLUME 1 – IN-DEPTH SESSIONS WITH A MASTER MUSICIAN

Homespun Listen & Learn Series

Mac "Dr. John" Rebennack, a veritable encyclopedia of music and lore, immerses you in all aspects of New Orleans boogie and blues piano. This intimate session with the legendary "Night Tripper" will help you build a solid repertoire and acquire a wealth of essential licks, runs, turnarounds, rhythms and techniques. Even non-players will love this guided tour of a great American tradition.

_______00699090 Book/CD Pack..................$19.95

EXPLORING BASIC BLUES FOR KEYBOARD

by Bill Boyd

This book introduces a blues scale system that produces idiomatic sounds characteristic of early blues, dixieland, boogie, swing and rock. Instruction begins with one-measure phrases followed by a step-by-step approach to twelve-measure improvisation.

_______00221029..$12.95

EXPLORING JAZZ SCALES FOR KEYBOARD

by Bill Boyd

Scales provide the basis for jazz improvisation and fill-ins. The scales presented in this book produce idiomatic sounds associated with many jazz styles. Boyd explores the jazz scales and examines their potential, giving the player more improvisation resources. Each chapter includes charts with the scales written in all keys with suggested fingerings and a list of chords which complement each scale. Music examples apply the scales to jazz chord progressions and compositions. Upon completion, the student will gain new insights into the practical application of jazz scales and will be able to enhance performance.

_______00221015..$12.95

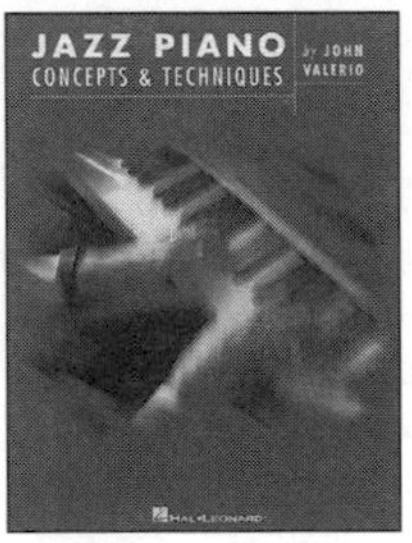

JAZZ PIANO – CONCEPTS & TECHNIQUES

by John Valerio

This book provides a step-by-step approach to learning basic piano realizations of jazz and pop tunes from lead sheets. Systems for voicing chords are presented from the most elementary to the advanced, along with methods for practicing each system. Both the non-jazz and the advanced jazz player will benefit from the focus on chords, chord voicings, harmony, melody and accompaniment, and styles.

_______00290490..$16.95

JAZZ RIFFS FOR PIANO

by Frank Feldman
Great Riffs Series
Cherry Lane Music

Learn the hottest tags, patterns, turnarounds, and solos in the style of the jazz world's legendary talents, such as Bud Powell, Thelonious Monk, George Shearing, Red Garland, Erroll Garner, Chick Corea, Bill Evans, and Keith Jarrett. Included in this book/audio package are detailed performance notes for all examples.

_______02503620 Book/CD Pack..................$17.95

THE POP PIANO BOOK

by Mark Harrison

A complete ground-up method for playing contemporary styles spontaneously on the keyboard. This 500-page book includes review of harmonic and rhythmic concepts, application of harmony to the keyboard in all keys, and then specific instruction for playing in pop, rock, funk, country, ballad, new age, and gospel styles. This unique book is endorsed by Grammy-winners and top educators. 498 pages

_______00220011..$39.95

THE SOURCE

by Steve Barta

Solid information regarding scales, chords, and how these two work together. The Source provides clear and complete right and left hand piano fingerings for scales, chords, and complete inversions. With over twenty different scales, each written in all twelve keys, The Source is the most complete collection of contemporary and traditional scales ever compiled into one book.

_______00240885..$12.95

THE ULTIMATE KEYBOARD CHORD BOOK

The Ultimate Keyboard Chord Book is a comprehensive volume containing over 1600 chord diagrams with 77 different chords for each key. Includes treble and bass clef notation for all chords in the book as well as a chord symbol chart. An introductory section explains the theory of chord construction.

_______00290045..$12.95

VOICINGS FOR JAZZ KEYBOARD

by Frank Mantooth

A respected soloist, clinician and writer, Mantooth has written this book for any keyboard player interested in developing better jazz chord voicing. Written more as a "how-to" book than a textbook, Voicings will make a valuable addition to the library of any performer, arranger, teacher or jazz theorist.

_______00855475..$12.95

Drum Reference, Instruction & Techniques

BASS DRUM CONTROL

by Colin Bailey

This perennial favorite among drummers helps players develop their bass drum technique and increase their flexibility through the mastery of exercises. Now available with CD.

_______06620020 Book/CD Pack $17.95

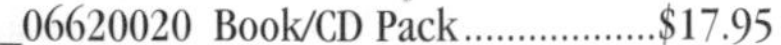

THE COMPLETE DRUMSET RUDIMENTS

by Peter Magadini

Use your imagination to incorporate these rudimental etudes into new patterns that you can apply to the drumset or tom toms as you develop your hand technique with the Snare Drum Rudiments, your hand and foot technique with the Drumset Rudiments and your polyrhythmic technique with the Polyrhythm Rudiments. The recording includes demonstrations of the rudiments and four drum solos utilizing all of the rudiments.

_______06620016 Book/CD Pack $14.95

CREATIVE TIMEKEEPING FOR THE CONTEMPORARY JAZZ DRUMMER

Rick Mattingly

Combining a variety of jazz ride cymbal patterns with coordination and reading exercises, *Creative Timekeeping* develops true independence: the ability to play any rhythm on the ride cymbal while playing any rhythm on the snare and bass drums. It provides a variety of jazz ride cymbal patterns as well as coordination and reading exercises that can be played along with them. Five chapters: Ride Cymbal Patterns; Coordination Patterns and Reading; Combination Patterns and Reading; Applications; and Cymbal Reading.

_______06621764...$8.95

THE DRUM PERSPECTIVE

by Peter Erskine
edited by Rick Mattingly

The Drum Perspective is like a series of private lessons that can be enjoyed anywhere, at any time. It is not written for drummers only, however! It is also designed for other instrumentalists and vocalists who work with drummers, bandleaders, educators and students of music, and anyone curious about the art of rhythm. This pack also includes a CD compilation of tracks that represent some of Erskine's best work, including: But Is It Art? • L.A. Stomp • Straphangin' • and more. Also includes transcriptions and charts of many of the CD performances, plus specific exercises designed to enhance a drummer's ability, creativity, and awareness.

_______06620015 Book/CD Pack $19.95

THE DRUMMER'S ALMANAC

by Jon Cohan

This celebration of the art of drumming is a must-have for all drummers, beginning to advanced. With essential tips on techniques and tongue-in-cheek anecdotes, *The Drummer's Almanac* is very informative and very fun. Includes lots of photographs, interviews, quotes, jokes, helpful hints, and more. Chapters include: A Short History of the Drum Set; A Natural Approach to Drumming by Dave Weckl; Care and Maintenance of Your Drums; A Day in the Life of Anton Fig; Some Handy Grooves; Drum Miking Basics; and much more!

_______00330237...$12.95

THE DRUMSET MUSICIAN

by Rod Morgenstein and Rick Mattingly

This beginning- to intermediate-level book contains hundreds of practical, usable beats and fills. It teaches how to apply a variety of patterns and grooves to the actual performance of songs. The CD includes demos and 14 play-along tracks covering rock, blues and pop styles, with detailed instructions on how to create exciting, solid drum parts. It's the most realistic – and fun! – way to learn drums.

_______06620011 Book/CD Pack $19.95

INNER RHYTHMS – MODERN STUDIES FOR SNARE DRUM

by Frank Colonnato

Inner Rhythms presents interesting and challenging etudes for snare drum based on the rhythms of contemporary music, including a variety of time signatures, shifting meters and a full range of dynamics. These studies will help improve reading skills as well as snare drum technique, and will provide insight to the rhythmic demands of modern music.

_______06620017...$7.95

JOE MORELLO – MASTER STUDIES

Modern Drummer Books

This is "the" book on hand development and drumstick control. *Master Studies* focuses on these important aspects: accent studies, buzz-roll exercises, single and double-stroke patterns, control studies, flam patterns, dynamic development, endurance studies, and much more!

_______06631474...$9.95

LEARN TO PLAY THE DRUMSET

by Peter Magadini

This method has been written to teach the basics of the drum set in the shortest amount of time. The method is unique in that it is a beginning course that starts the student out on the entire drum set.

_______06620000 Book One..........................$5.95
_______06620002 Book One/Cassette Pak.....$12.95
_______06620001 Book Two..........................$5.95
_______06620005 Book Two/Cassette Pak.....$12.95
_______06620050 Spanish Edition $4.95

METHOD BOOK 1

by Blake Neely & Rick Mattingly

In this beginner's guide to drums, you'll learn music notation, riffs and licks, syncopation, rock, blues and funk styles, and improvisation. Includes over 75 songs and examples.

_______00697285 Book/CD Pack...................$7.95

MODERN PERCUSSION GROOVES

by Glen Caruba
Centerstream Publishing

Glen Caruba's first book, Afro-Cuban Drumming, touched on basic Latin percussion styles. This follow-up teaches how to incorporate these traditional rhythms and techniques into modern pop and rock playing. Covers instrument playing tips (congas, bongo, timbale, cowbell, shakers and more), funk grooves, pop ballads, Afro-Cuban 6/8, jazz-fusion grooves, cha-cha pop, and lots more. The CD features 40 tracks of examples.

_______00000228 Book/CD Pack $16.95

NEW DIRECTIONS AROUND THE DRUMS

by Mark Hamon
Centerstream Publications

Endorsed by noteables like Hal Blain, Peter Erskine, Jim Chapin, and more, this book features a comprehensive, non-rudimental approach to the drumset for beginners to professionals! It combines straight drum-to-drum patterns with cross-sticking configurations, and includes open-ended free-style drum patterns for use as solos and fills.

_______00000170...$14.95

Vocal Publications

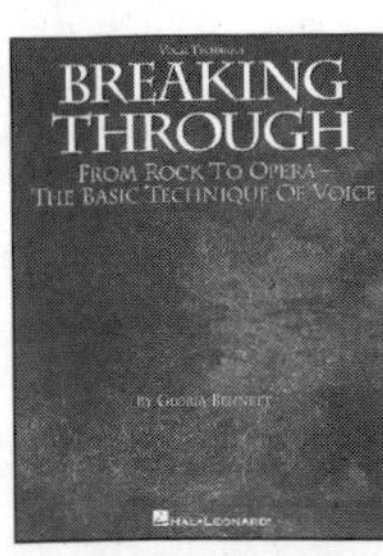

BREAKING THROUGH

From Rock To Opera – The Basic Technique Of Voice
by Gloria Bennett

Author and voice teacher Gloria Bennett has taught Axl Rose of Guns N'Roses, Dexter of Offspring, and Anthony Kiedis of the Red Hot Chili Peppers, and others. Her comprehensive and practical book offers a clear explanation of the voice as an instrument, and proper vocal technique. Through examples, anecdotes, and exercises, *Breaking Through* provides for both the novice and professional vocalist a vital sourcebook for maintaining and enhancing the quality of the voice., 8-1/2" x 11"

______00330258 ....$14.95

LEARN TO SING HARMONY

taught by Cathy Fink, Marcy Marxer, Robin and Linda Williams
Homespun

Four wonderful singers teach beginners or experienced singers the principles of two-, three-, and four-part harmonies to enhance favorite folk, country, and bluegrass songs. A special feature: the parts are recorded on separate stereo tracks for practicing with either the melody or the harmony line. Teaches 20 songs.

______00641424 Book/3-CD Pack..............$34.95

THE PROFESSIONAL SINGER'S HANDBOOK

by Gloria Rusch

This book realistically prepares a singer for life in the world of professional music. Author Gloria Rusch gives candid advice on a wide range of topics and includes extensive interviews with Kevon Edmonds of the group After 7, stage and television producer Ken Kragen, Janis Siegel of Manhattan Transfer, multi-platinum songwriter Andy Goldmark, and other knowledgeable session singers, sound engineers, and arrangers.

______00330349..$19.95

SINGING JAZZ

The Singers and Their Styles
by Bruce Crowther and Mike Pinfold
Miller Freeman Books

This book explores the lives, work and music of vocalists past and present to portray the diverse and stimulating world of the jazz singer. Includes: illuminating profiles of legendary artists, including Billie Holiday, Ella Fitzgerald, Sarah Vaughn, Carmen McRae, Louis Armstrong and many more; insights from contemporary masters about the ups and downs of jazz singing today; and A-Z reference section of capsule biographies and essential recording for over 200 singers; a photo section; and lots more.

______00330391..$17.95

PROFESSIONAL SINGER'S POP/ROCK FAKE BOOK

There's never been such a singer-friendly fake book! Songs include material from the entire rock era, with ballads as well as many uptempo dance tunes. Over 100 songs every singer needs, in appropriate keys, with intros, interludes, endings and background vocal harmonies – giving singers performable, complete versions of each song. Includes: Beautiful in My Eyes • Blue Suede Shoes • Can You Feel the Love Tonight • Don't Let Me Be Lonely Tonight • Fields of Gold • Great Balls of Fire • Imagine • In My Life • Just the Way You Are • The Loco-Motion • Somewhere Out There • Stand by Me • Tears in Heaven • Time After Time • Twist and Shout • Unchained Melody • Under the Boardwalk • Your Song • and more. Each edition also has songs which are gender-specific.

______00240091 Men's Edition $19.95
______00240090 Women's Edition..............$19.95

THE SINGER'S MOVIE ANTHOLOGY

compiled by Richard Walters

A terrific, unprecedented collection of over 50 songs written for and sung in the movies, with a completely different selection of songs for women and men singers. The songs are presented in the original sheet music editions. Each volume includes historical and plot notes about each movie represented.

WOMEN'S EDITION

56 songs including: Beauty and the Beast • Isn't It Romantic? • It Might As Well Be Spring • Let Yourself Go • The Man That Got Away • Maybe This Time • On the Good Ship Lollipop • When I Fall in Love • and more.

______00747076 ....$19.95

MEN'S EDITION

55 songs, including: Bella Notte • Easy to Love • I've Got My Love to Keep Me Warm • If I Had a Talking Picture of You • In the Still of the Night • The Way You Look Tonight • When You Wish Upon a Star • and more.

______00747069...$19.95

STANDARD BALLADS

Cabaret arrangements for singer and trio (piano, bass, drums) with a companion CD of performances and accompaniments

Fantastic songs in fantastic renditions, in comfortable keys for pop singing. Contents: All the Things You Are • Autumn Leaves • Call Me Irresponsible • East of the Sun • I Left My Heart in San Francisco • I'll Be Seeing You • In a Sentimental Mood • Isn't It Romantic? • The Very Thought of You • The Way You Look Tonight. Book/CD Packages.

______00740088 Women's Edition $19.95
______00740089 Men's Edition $19.95

10 POPULAR WEDDING DUETS

with a companion CD

10 duets for the wedding. The companion CD contains two performances of each song, one with singers, the other is the orchestrated instrumental track for accompaniment. Contents: All I Ask of You • Annie's Song • Don't Know Much • Endless Love • I Swear • In My Life • Let It Be Me • True Love • Up Where We Belong • When I Fall in Love.

______00740002 Book/CD package............$19.95

10 WEDDING SOLOS

with a companion CD

A terrific, useful collection of 10 songs for the wedding, including both popular songs and contemporary Christian material. There are two versions of each song on the companion CD, first with full performances with singers, then with the instrumental accompaniments only. Contents: Here, There and Everywhere • I Swear • The Promise • Someone Like You • Starting Here Starting Now • God Causes All Things to Grow • Parent's Prayer • This Is the Day • Wedding Prayer • Where There Is Love.

______00740004 High Voice Book/CD pkg...$19.95
______00740009 Low Voice Book/CD pkg....$19.95

90001410